How to Hug a Light Being

A Spiritual Journey

by Janet E. Swartz

CREDITS
Cover design: Paul J. Morehead, Jr.
Pages typography: Paul Siemsen

ISBN-13: 978-0-578-65343-3

How to Hug a Light Being: A Spiritual Journey

DEDICATION

*I dedicate this book to my son, Daniel,
now off the planet, who offered healing
to so many while he was here, and
is now the vehicle for my own, and
perhaps your healing of loss.*

ACKNOWLEDGEMENTS

I offer heartfelt gratitude to those who have inspired, loved and supported me in my great adventure of life on the planet,

— to my wonderful ever patient and loving husband Fred, who spent many hours with me discussing the concepts and clarity of the book's presentation, not to mention the hours of love and support through our decades of marriage,

— to our daughter Deborah, physical, spiritual and emotional healer, advocate for indigenous peoples, and perfect reflection of the Divine who always brings me to my highest,

— to everyone who offered their editing expertise with special thanks to Demerie Faitler, Leslee Goldstein, Deborah Swartz, Laure Reminick, Kate Ross,

— to all my clients and students who continue to give me the opportunity to grow in my own evolution and skills and abilities to assist them on their path through personal transformation,

— to the magic of transformation itself sourcing from Divine intelligence and to the human condition that can create positive change and self-healing,

— to Maharishi Mahesh Yogi who gave me a spiritual technique for spiritual regeneration,

— and to Dan for the inspiration to understand what it means to be human in this time and space and to know that there is a bigger realm that is waiting and ready for us at the appropriate time.

How to Hug a Light Being
A Spiritual Journey
By Janet Swartz

TABLE OF CONTENTS

TABLE OF CONTENTS (Continued)

Preface

I imagine that a mother's greatest fear is losing a child.

It was definitely mine from the time I gave birth. Inevitably, we are delivered opportunities to overcome our fears.

Such an opportunity presented itself to me when my first born, my only son, committed suicide at age twenty-five. He was smart, handsome, kind, compassionate, clever and talented — so loved by me, his Dad and his many friends and clientele.

This book shares my process of coming to terms with what seemed at first like the harshest of realities. How one chooses to die is a phenomenon that may or may not be a real choice. Illness, accident, natural disaster, war…it all rests in the hands that may not be our own. But what about those who do take it in their own hands. Is that a choice? After a lengthy introspection, my awareness has come to a peaceful recognition that it has served as a great blessing.

I am able to acknowledge my son's death as the perfect closure for his life. Not only was it perfectly suited for his inevitable destiny, but it was also the most evolutionary experience for me as well as for his father, sister, and his wide outreach of friends, acquaintances and those he mentored.

We came to know the truest essence of Dan after his passing. As we continue to learn the many facets of his life and soul purpose, we continue to learn of our own. We became aware of the immortality imbedded in the mortality, in the greater purpose inherent in what seems to be purposelessness, and in the acceptance of the perfection of all things. The recognition of who Dan became and recognized in himself as a sentient Being is part of what has inspired this book.

I didn't want to write a story that elicits fear, disbelief, sadness, or undue compassion toward me. Perhaps that is why I spent a year and a half talking to people so they could see that I was ok. I learned that they, too, gained relief. It is not meant to be a therapeutic thesis, but an inspirational and fascinating story that I felt compelled to write.

My goal in sharing this personal tale is to help alleviate anyone's suffering over losing a child or loved one. Grief inevitably accompanies loss and transforming that grief seems to be the inescapable challenge of being human.

Time does heal

Time does heal, and continues to create new, expanded perspectives. If time is relative, and healing can take place in a moment, the time-frame for healing must be very different for everyone.

As Dan's Dad gently placed his hand on Dan's lifeless shoulder, he realized that he couldn't call back spirit, he blessed him and let him go in love. He never felt the loss nor the distance as a barrier to his relationship of having a son. I, who wasn't willing to go to Dan's house when I was suspecting the worst, had to go through anger, forgiveness, and intense grief in order to rest peacefully in that love. My healing necessitated spending time alone, and then, explaining to others who Dan, the light being, really was. His sister, who had to break into his house only to find his lifeless body, took a few years away from home to eventually regain a deep feeling of inner love in order to fully heal.

Our own projection and timing for healing a painful loss requires that we create new patterns in our existence. For me, accepting the designation of the mother of a son who committed suicide didn't feel appropriate or fair to me. I never thought this would be a reality for me to live out. Yet, to explain Dan as an avatar who never took drugs, medication, or alcohol, doesn't necessarily make it easier for those who are dealing with their kids who do use these methods to deal with life's challenges. Life is precious, and who are we to judge what is right or wrong for someone?

So, let's just consider that this is my story, the story of this Light Being's Mom. The perspective may be quite different from yours, or even members of my own family. However, if there are messages for you, some heartfelt understandings that help you in your life or in the lives of those you feel close to, that is all that I could hope for.

Why this book was not hard to write.

I have to say that when the time is right, it IS right. The writing of this book flowed through my fingers as fast as I could type. If I hadn't needed to eat and sleep and attend to my responsibilities, I could have just allowed the words to come without interruption.

I was often asked if it was emotionally difficult to address the subject of Dan, his leaving, and his legacy. The question would always surprise me. I guess losing a son to suicide held an inherent definition of tragedy, something going wrong. There seemed to be an assumption that he must have been suffering, and that I continue to grieve.

As a practical matter, through the experience, I am exploring my own understanding of who I am, as Janet -- my Beingness, separate from my story. Part of my life's story has taken shape through Daniel's beliefs, understandings, and experiences with himself, me and others. Such a life-changing event has served as a self-reflective learning for my own life's journey. I have come to understand that motherhood and Self-hood, are states of non-attachment, which I believe is a truth of our existence.

This writing comes at a time when I am out of the mode of attempting to "fix" others. Being an intuitive and facilitator of a transformational healing process that I actually developed at Dan's prompting, I offer my tools to those who ask. My life's learning continues every day, and I often find my growth experiences to be extraordinary. I hope to humbly share some of that in this book. In the words of the Sufi master Nawad Jan-Sishan Kahn, "a candle is not here to illuminate itself."

I appreciated, and still do, all the love, compassion, and support lavished on me during the days of integrating a new reality. It did take a few months of inward time to heal. Many people who projected their sorrow and fear would exclaim, "I don't know how you can be ok," or "I could never imagine losing a child." Of course, it is absolutely true that others couldn't imagine this for themselves. It was not meant for their learning this lifetime. We all have our own road to travel, our own karmic events to work out. I couldn't imagine that type of loss for them, either. And, I never felt, nor do I feel now, any envy toward those who have a beautiful son to love who is in the flesh. My love remains an undying connection to Dan that still has never left from the day he was born.

It has always been clear to me that I could never have lost a young child. Such an event would have been devastating and not an easy one to heal. When Dan left the body, he was an adult with whom I had developed a close relationship, understanding, and mutual mentoring. That was my experience. And, he did make his own choice. When I talk to those who lost babies or young children, they most often describe their spiritual learning—or gifting, as it is sometimes referred to — which served as a means for healing.

We are all seeking joy, to live in the continuous moment of Bliss and feel that all "is right with the world." As my spiritual teacher would say, it's better to be a knower of reality than a seeker, but, of course, we all have to start somewhere. What's better than now? How and when we receive the knowledge needed to experience our truth depends on our openness and timing. Then the messages are relevant and serve a purpose for our evolution.

I share my journey in the hopes it will help others on their own.

I believe this is the ultimate blessing of my son's life and death.

From Khalil Gibran's, 'On Children' in "The Prophet"

Your children are not your children.
They are the sons and daughters of Life's longing
for itself.
They come through you but not from you,
And though they are with you yet they belong
not to you.
You may give them your love but not your thoughts,
For they have their own thoughts.
You may house their bodies but not their souls,
For their souls dwell in the house of tomorrow,
which you cannot visit, not even in your dreams.
You may strive to be like them,
but seek not to make them like you.
For life goes not backward nor tarries with yesterday.
You are the bows from which your children as living
arrows are sent forth.
Let you bending in the archer's hand be for gladness.

———————

Chapter 1

Introducing the Light Being

Sometimes I cry, but mostly I don't. The communication, which we received shortly after he vanished from the planet, was "please honor the way I left. It will give me peace."

What more does a mother want than for her child to be happy.

He wasn't actually a child. An almost twenty-six-year old, he was a strapping young man of six feet, four inches in bare feet. Why I was the mother of a son who couldn't hold the earth energy in a larger-than-life spiritual body is really the question.

One cannot ask why someone was or is the way they are. It just is. I spent much of Dan's twenty-five years trying to change the environment so he'd be happy. And, in the last few months, I continued to seek ways to help him stay here, holding on tightly to my own energy when I witnessed him receding.

A few months before he left, Dan shared, with bent head, soft mannerism, and humble heart, that he was an avatar. When I asked what that was, he just simply said, a level of light being.

It was hard for me to ask more at this point, as it had been in other situations that year. I couldn't bear the thought of what he was truly thinking. He had mentioned one day that he'd never need us to buy him another car. He was given one as a present after graduation and his stint in law school. At this point in his life, he was gainfully employed as a Junior Accountant for his Dad's small public accounting firm. Daniel, or Dan as his friends called him, only said he'd never need another one. My assumption was that he'd most likely be able to pay for it himself, but I detected a deeper meaning. I wanted to ask what he was thinking, but I held it in. Or, maybe I didn't, and said, "Why would you say that." I don't remember.

He also said he would probably never marry his beloved girlfriend. They had been together over three years and were friends before that, and enjoyed doing spiritual work together. To this day, she still has a regular communication with him whenever she chooses to check in. When I asked her most recent partner if he minded that she continues to have this relationship with Dan, he said without hesitation, "No, he helps her a lot." I thought that to be a very big-hearted answer. That was comforting to me for sure, and I adore the fellow. I said to her, I think Dan would approve of your boyfriend. She promptly retorted, "What do you mean approve, he organized it."

Yes, Dan organized it all. He paid his bills, cleaned the little house he lived in, and left during a storm so no one could hear the gun shot. He had taken a break from his job after completing tax season on April 15. It was now passing mid-May.

During the Memorial Service, on Memorial Day of 2010, those who could "see," envisioned him with spread wings encompassing the enormous tent. He was heading up a council of Beings and appeared to be in charge of what turned out to be a beautiful, heartfelt, and healing event for well over three hundred and fifty people. Our backyard was filled with people, angels, and a divine presence that is truly impossible to set to words.

Chapter 2

The Beginning: Birth and Love

Birthing is probably the most painful and yet heart expanding experience that anyone could ever ask for. That is certainly true if Mom is prepared to take on her role without pain killers and medical intervention that precludes any experience at all.

Common in my mother's generation, the preferred style of child birth was to literally knock the birther out. The doc, nurse, or staff member would be the one to receive the once protected, in-utero Being who emerged into a cold, rough, and seemingly unsafe world. Maybe the first cries of a baby were a relief for the medical staff, but I imagine that the newborn was having a rather different, even shocking experience. (Perhaps this isn't the case with C-sections. I haven't investigated the preplanned or emergency births where a mother is cut open to relieve mom and baby of the forceful, heavy contractions and a medically unassisted birthing canal experience.)

I had made my to-do list, or rather a NOT-to-do list, for the birthing center staff in preparation for a natural childbirth. That included: no medication, no monitoring equipment, and no taking the baby away after birth to weigh in. It was a challenge to keep this agreement in force, as I was a very loud deliverer. With each contraction I hollered, and the nurse kept invading with pills in hand. After shooing her out for the umpteenth time, my husband, aka coach, put a "do not disturb sign" on the door. It worked! No more interruptions. I later learned that one could release the unbearable physical tension through toning, a much more mellifluous way to greet a birthing baby. It must have been quite a night for my husband having to listen to all of this for eight hours.

Although it felt that my labor went on forever, it was apparently not really that long. Eight hours isn't considered long in the birthing world. I've heard so many stories of a hard three-day labor by women who stuck out the natural childbirth scene and lived to tell their story. Yet, for me, it felt interminable, until it was time to push.

In spite of my reticence, when the time did come, the doc managed to talk me into an episiotomy, another thing on my not-to-do list. How needless. Daniel, as we were already calling him, came out without a hitch. Only fifteen minutes of a love experience that I had never before been blessed with. Once the doctor was willing to wake up in the middle of this night and be on duty, my body heaved out one final effort in the midst of, "I love you, I love you, I love you." The words continued in a flow of hyper-blissful expectancy, culminating in final physical relief.

Ready to coddle our new baby boy, (yes, it was a boy as I had thought) and bond together as we swaddled him in a warm blanket, we welcomed this new soul into the world with silence and then stories of a divinely human life. Then, to our amazement, with focused attention, Daniel interlaced his fingers (not a common ability at this stage of development), struck a thoughtful pose, looked to the left, then to the right, and let out a yell that seemed to spread throughout the entire Universe. What went through his mind was not evident, but we can guess that he was wondering what he'd bargained for by coming into a human body.

Suddenly, a flurry of movement disrespectfully interrupted our nurturing flow. A nurse, appearing out of nowhere, whisked our little one away before we knew what had happened. Daniel was quickly unwrapped from his warm blanket, placed naked on the cold scale as he belted out the words, "no, no, no." I imagine by now he was in total disbelief of his new physical reality. He weighed in at six pound and fifteen ounces. And I, not being a small woman, was unnecessarily cut and had to give up my baby to a cold scale. I was pissed.

Once he was back in my arms, I felt a relief and relaxation that it was over. There he was, beautiful and perfect, and he, too, began to settle down. Completely exhausted, I just wanted to sleep. And without seeking permission from others or myself, I was out.

Fred held his first-born close, and explained to him the nature of living a divine life on the planet with spiritual guides to help him at every stage.

Given that everything did go fine, I probably could have had a home birth, which we had prepared for. But since we lived in an apartment with adjoining neighbors, it is just as well since I was such a noisy birther. "Just in case," or "what if," or "I'm new at this," were all my reasons for being in a hospital.

Chapter 3:

My Personality Challenges —
Prelude To Early Days With Dan

————————————————

Learning to be present with the Self, staying centered within life's ebb and flow seems to be a spiritual exercise for the seeker. If we believe we are made in God's image and aspire to that refined potential of perfection, it seems that we have a responsibility to develop positive ways of thinking and behaving. Asking oneself, "Am I separate or one with my Creator?" is a good question and can be answered as long there is a willingness to surrender the needs and demands of the small ego. The conundrum is, "If 'I' am not in charge of my life, then who is?"

Being a Mom, a camp counselor in my earlier days, school teacher, and daughter of a controlling-type of mother, I really had to look at "control." In my case, it really came down to self-control in the sense that my responses to challenges were not always gentle or even kind. "Give it up" would have been a perfect edict to live by. A phrase that comes to mind is, "Just come back to your center, the place of calm and peace." I heard Dan once say to me, frustrated as he recognized the intensity of my inner battles, "you'd be better off living alone." That brought me to my senses, at least temporarily, I'm sure.

Growing up with God and moving on

As a young girl, I never thought much about being other than an earthling. I did feel a Divine presence within me, whom I called God. It was a belief system my Dad must have taught me and was innocently acknowledged as a felt experience. I knew that I was never alone. Therefore, praying to someone elsewhere was ok, but directly connecting to God for me was better. I always felt surrounded and protected by a non-physical, higher Being whom I could talk to anytime. This ephemeral friend was part of me and special to me, and always available. I recognized that I was more than just a physical being in this rather awkward looking body.

I don't know if I thought consciously about being protected all the time, but I just assumed that was the case, so I was quite adventurous in my path on the planet.

More knowledge of who I was and who I was becoming came with my meditation teacher, Maharishi Mahesh Yogi in 1973. I was given a technique to transcend my relative, ever-changing nature, my emotional fears and negative tendencies as well as my physicality. The simple, natural, mental technique of Transcendental Meditation gave me the tool to expand my awareness on a daily basis and live in a wider arena than what was directly in front of my eyes.

Maharishi provided vocabulary to describe higher states of consciousness and how they might manifest. It is this knowledge that helped me not only begin to understand my own growth, but also to comprehend Dan's experiences. Whether I subscribed to Dan's thinking about being unable to contain the dense earthly energy or not, his writings clearly indicated his development and expressions of higher states.

Ask and you shall receive

As is true with so many of us, we always want answers. Although it was clear to me that the "whys" of our life's events may never become apparent, I really wanted to understand how the feeling responses to the "whats" of situations could be transformed and healed. A deep understanding of the nature of positive transformation came to me years ago. I developed a process that offers a powerful way to fulfill energy shifts for positive transformation, which I have now trademarked as The Empowerment Process.

Many years ago while my kids were young and I was embarking on the healer path, I asked Nature to give me more understanding of inter-dimensional life. I didn't really know what I was asking for, but many of my clients seemed to need greater clarity of where they came from as well as where they were going. So it seemed like a reasonable request. I was already able to receive pertinent information regarding peoples' past lives if they needed to know anything for their healing in the present, but this was different.

I also noticed that I could interpret planetary information if necessary without being an astrologer. One of my intuitive friends discerned that I was able to reside on the inter-dimensional plane and be in many places at once. Although this information was mysterious to me, I guess it explains how I am able to work with others who are connected to realms beyond their physical existence. Although I wasn't able to keep Dan here, I was given insight into a soul's existence without a gross material body.

As a consequence of Dan taking his life, others were given the somewhat difficult yet necessary task to understand and integrate the shocking event. People could easily open their hearts to me, and the opportunity for a joint healing would take place. What was deemed a tragedy opened a channel for not only healing the heart, but adventuring into possibilities of a new belief system.

Chapter 4

Deborah's Presence

Nearly three years after Daniel's entrance to this world, I was blessed with another child, a daughter, whom we named Deborah. The journey for her began easily. She delivered herself with just my husband officiating. I wanted to be in the safe warm space of our new home, in the company of only my husband and midwife. I arranged for Daniel to go to a friend's house as I didn't know what to expect. As it turned out, the entire event did prove to be calm, serene, easy, quick and perfect. All that came to be as hoped for, except without the midwife.

My husband was the coach, receiver, and first to hold our new perfect little girl who slid out within an hour. Our midwife, still finishing her shower sixty miles away, showed up in time to clean up. I figured if animals could fulfill this mission alone in the woods, I should be able to handle this without the help of medical staff. The independent streak in me was assisted by my calm, fearless, capable husband who blessed the event. We were prepared this time!

Once Daniel came home that afternoon, he insisted on holding his new sister. It seemed like a very long time later that I was given the opportunity to take her from this loving protector and tend to her myself. We all needed our chance for bonding.

The easy beginning took a turn a few years later.

When Deborah was five, she went through a medical crisis of no small proportion. Her discomfort of increasing back aches and stomach aches brought us to many doctors and healers before we could discover the problem. A family friend and pediatrician who laid his hand on her abdomen sent us to the hospital immediately. The MRI's gave us the results. She was carrying a football-size tumor on her left kidney and several more golf ball sized masses that had metastasized to her lungs. It had already developed into advanced stage-four kidney cancer.

I spent the night in the waiting room in anguish and trepidation as the decision to cut her open for a biopsy was made. I was certain they would just take "it" out and we would be done. Not so. A two-and-a-half year protocol with a cocktail of chemotherapies, several surgeries and radiation therapy followed.

The blessing of Daniel's love during that time was apparent. He completely cooperated with overnights away from home, something he had never been willing to do at other times. When his sister came out of her surgeries, he was always there to greet her and welcome her back. His heart was always so tender towards her.

It took Deborah a while to expose the evidence of her cross-body scars in a bikini, but moving to Hawaii cured her of what had been formally an embarrassment. She was able to accept it as part of her natural beauty. Like accepting the body scars, we observed that she was also able to accept the "mental scars" of having to go through such difficult health challenges. She recognized and accepted that she was surrounded by lots of love and support, and the outcome justified the experiences she had to go through. This would be a recurrent theme in her life, and a training ground which helped shape her courage and acceptance for events still in her future destiny. We never know why things happen as they do, but in hindsight, we can appreciate how one event serves as preparation for the next in so many ways.

Deborah's Independent Educational Path

Deborah always had independent and interesting pursuits which are still guiding her into adulthood. At age sixteen, she traveled alone to France to master the language in its own environment, at nineteen she left for a summer to live and work in Maui, and at age twenty-two she was off to New Zealand for some exceptional experiences with extraordinary healers. Her first two years at Wheaton College in Massachusetts studying Anthropology and Ethnomusicology were followed by independently designed educational programs that would support her interest in intercultural spiritual studies. Her need to travel the globe in pursuit of those studies was a prerequisite for her driven destiny to connect with extraordinary healers and spiritual mentors. She was independently creating her own unique life journey.

This included connecting with the Maoris in New Zealand, Native American Indian Shamans in the American Southwest, and renowned Holy Men in Maui. One exceptional Maori Holy Man allowed her, (an unusual exception made for this young white girl), to walk along with him and nine other "kiwis" bare-footed through the mountains on meaningful and transformational spiritual quests.

As she left for each of these journeys, I recognized feeling the same trepidation that had beset me when she went into surgeries as a little girl. This was another test for me in the training camp of detachment and acceptance of my child's independent life decisions. It was always my desire to support my children's choices, but it was never easy. I had no idea how much harder it could get.

Chapter 5

My Early Days As The Protector

I always felt compelled to stay vigilant to keep Daniel safe. As I look back, I realize that from day one I was protective and carried a general concern about losing him. At the one-year-old-birthday parties when he wasn't yet walking, I'd do my best to keep him out of harm's way from the unstable steps of toddlers. As time went on, I noticed I would actually try to change the environment in order to keep him happy, or at least comfortable. It didn't always work, and later on, he just told me that it disempowered him. I guess it was my own need for emotional protection.

Dan did not make my inability to "let it be" an easy burden. As an infant, he would wail whenever I tried to put him down for a nap or when I'd just need a physical reprieve from holding him. I remember having to carry him in a baby backpack while I vacuumed the house. It was as if I had a little supervisor that I had to lug around all the time. I didn't seem to be willing to let him slug it out alone.

The only one who could successfully lay him down for a nap

was a teenage helper who reportedly had some practice with a baby brother. I do imagine, however, that I did have to let him holler whenever I took my shower or needed to use the toilet.

At night, I lay beside him, nursing every two hours for twenty minutes at a time. My nights felt very long. At seventeen months, my milk was his total sustenance, and I was told by the Ayurvedic physicians to start to wean him. Start and end was the way it went; cold turkey. Dad took over for three sleepless nights offering him cooked pear and some kind of cereal. Pablum was not his preference, and I laid awake wondering if he would ever quit the commotion.

The technique worked, however, and I replaced my breast milk with bottled milk that he voraciously consumed along with a bit of food. He got a little bigger even though he was next to the smallest and the lightest when he went off to school. On the lower third of the medical weight and size chart, I was stymied as to why an Eastern astrologer said he would be a big fellow when he grew up. "Tall and skinny," I imagined. But the answer was always "big."

The astrological projection did play out. He grew through three pant sizes during his thirteenth year. Finally, he stopped growing at six feet four inches.

Highs

It wasn't just his physique that was growing in leaps and bounds. His off-body-energy continued to expand at an almost unmanageable rate.

His experience as a Bar Mitzvah boy standing on the synagogue pulpit caused such an expansion, I wasn't sure Daniel would be able to stay grounded enough and in his body to proceed. Fortunately, our gifted friend Kaitlin was present, and took up the charge to keep him standing and centered so he could complete this spiritual rite of passage.

I don't think Daniel minded being brought up Jewish. He also had continuing exposure to Hindu philosophy through Maharishi's teaching, which labeled us as "HinJews." Yet it wasn't about religion. It was about expansion of consciousness, having true perceptual changes that made Maharishi's quote, "knowledge is structured in consciousness," reality's blessing.

What came as an unexpected eye opener for me was when I realized that I had a kid who was telepathic, empathic, and connected to Mother Divine. My own experiences were very different than his. It felt quite daunting to realize that he could read my thoughts. He always knew what was going on.

Dan's inside haven

I love being outdoors. Gardening, walking in the woods, biking and swimming not only gives me a chance to move my body for health and well-being, boosting my endorphins, but also gives me a sense of belonging to the Earth. Since it was nearly impossible to get Dan outside as a little boy, I felt cooped up much of the time. I noticed how I how I would try to stick it out longer when he would complain about my being in the garden too long. He would either cry for me to go inside, or call me in a rather freaked out tone from inside to come in NOW.

And, forget any walks. Even a stroller was not enticing, interesting, or compelling in any way for Daniel. The bicycle seat I bought for him never got used. You can take a horse to water, but you can't make him drink. The fact that he would go in our woods and play with his friend, Avi, always amazed me.

One day, two young brothers came over to play with Daniel. They went out to our back yard where they had permission to play on the little beach area by our pond. I do admit that I always trusted Daniel and his friends to not wander into the water unattended. I never had a problem. When the boys came back after a time, the brothers were covered in mud while Dan was spick and span. Not a drop of dirt on him. I wondered if they played in the same place even though I knew that they were together in our backyard. My washer and drier came in handy, and the boys were happily distracted playing with their friend's favorite fantasy, super hero games.

Playing in his fantasy world

Playing "men" kept Daniel busy for hours. He would often ask me to join in the grandeur, but I usually answered, "I don't know how to play your games."

When I would try, he would feel satisfied that I would just follow his lead. I am embarrassed to admit that I was not much into fantasy games, books, or movies. I guess I was not a playmate for him; too serious. Even my elderly Dad pushing through his late eighties enjoyed reading the Harry Potter series, watching the Star Wars adventures and even listening to Dan's music until the time of his own passing.

Although Dan and I had made a few pacts that we would help each other in our respective evolutions, the challenge was a difficult one for me. As I continued to learn who Dan was and his preferences for living his life, I began to realize that every step that seemed difficult for him was also difficult for me. Something had to change.

So, as an adult who had realized himself, at least to a degree that he felt he knew who he was, Dan helped me begin to operate differently. He kept gifting me this way. Our walk-and-talks were completely enjoyable. I often asked him to verify that he was speaking from personal experience as his descriptions of consciousness were generally something I had only read about. He was so other-worldly. Once I started to really listen and believe him, he began to open up. I learned so much about him, about different realities, and consequently, more about myself.

Conquering fears

I related to Dan as mother to son. He went from a very little guy to a very big physical being. Once he completed his tallness, he just continued to gain the weight necessary to keep him from being called tall and skinny. Now he was just big. The leftover physical proofs of a very quick growth were the stretch marks on his torso and butt that took a few years to blend in and disappear.

When I noticed that he would sometimes hang his head, cowering to minimize his "tallness," it would bother me. I think he felt that appearing a little shorter helped him be less intrusive. When asked, he told me it was a way to pull in the enormous energy of his looming presence. He explained that he carried a humility this way, and how important humility was. If that was his way of appearing humble, I didn't like it.

He always said we have to conquer our greatest fears. They would just melt and dissipate, and we would be so much bigger than they were. As a mother, my biggest fear was losing a child. I always felt to be careful with him. He would just say to me to let go, and when I did, I lost my child. I know now that releasing one's biggest fear can become one's greatest blessing. Life in this human body does go on, and I personally must not be finished!

I suspect Dan's possible fear of leaving the body and anything here that he may have felt attached to was an unexpected emotion. Dealing with an emotional body was not something he had apparently been used to but had to contend with. Maybe he conquered his own biggest fear in making this transition. I think he is hoping we can all have an easy time letting go when the time comes. I certainly hope leaving the body is easy… it will happen when the time is right, whenever that is. And, I, "the controller," certainly will not be in charge.

Chapter 6

Making A Pact

When Daniel was about four, I remember making a necessary pact with him. He always insisted on wearing his superman outfit day after day. That meant wearing underwear over his blue sweat pants. When I had to go to the grocery store, with his little sister in my arms, he refused to take off the outside underwear. I wish I didn't care, but at the time, I seemed adamant that this young boy be presentable for the public.

Frustrated at my attempts to explain all this, one day I made him promise to sit on the couch and not move a muscle while I went grocery shopping with his little sister. He did promise, and actually kept it, a trait that he continued during his life here. But, I was a wreck while I was gone, leaving a four-year-old like that. I guess it is too late to be arrested for child neglect! He was actually fine.

When I came home, I burst into tears in relief, and talked non-stop for maybe a half-hour about my "mommying" frustrations. I can't imagine it was easy for either kid to listen to this ranting, but Dan and I made a pact. He would help me with my emotional frustrations, and I would try to not interfere with his antics. It sort of worked, but you'll make your own assessment.

This concept of a pact, came up again when, in desperation, I needed him to not sit on the couch all summer doing nothing. My husband and I decided to send Daniel to camp. He was about ten years old, and we chose a place near my folks in North Carolina. We thought some physical exercise and outdoor activity would benefit his soul.

The entire month, I was battling anxiety. The camp didn't want us to call and speak with him, only connect through letters. And, yet, I was feeling his feelings of discontent in the camp arena. I, myself, loved going away from my parents for a month during the summer, out of the clutches of my Mom's emotional waves and sometimes insensitive attention.

So, one day, the camp director did call, and reported that Daniel sprained an ankle and that he was being cared for by the local infirmary. I then got to speak with him, and knew the emotional suffering he must be going through. He said that he was ok, though. He had made a pact with God agreeing to get physically hurt in exchange for releasing his emotional pain. I was actually relieved that it was only a sprain that seemed to do the trick.

I rejoiced when that summer was over, and I wondered if we had made a mistake in sending him away. Yet, there were more camps ahead, and the future camp experiences as a teen were a great boon for his theater stardom and the making of close friendships.

Chapter 7

His Energy
— Anything is possible

The intensity with which Dan lived was beyond my own comprehension. He displayed it, sometimes as anger. I imagine it was a driving force in his quickly expanding energetic life. His musical life proved to be a great outlet with some extreme expressions of emotion. They were powerful, and usually tasteful. The adjective "smashing" from the group "Smashing Pumpkins," which he enjoyed playing on his electric guitar, gives you the idea of the energy behind his feelings. Mostly raging, symphonic, and energetically extreme, some of this group's expressions also elicited a contrasting energy, a soft and soothing experience. Dan picked up this mode in his original musical creation, "Crystal Echoes."

Dan's fervent energy was kept private and at bay most of the time. In general, people saw him as a sensitive and sweet soul, always shining love from his eyes. Both personality traits were true.

Once he left, Fred and I went through the mass of disheveled papers in his closet uncovering some very telling pieces that he had written in high school. At that time he was still learning who he was, what his essence and energy was about. The following high school writing assignment where he was to journal, "What is your most powerful gift?" gives a glimpse into his nature.

My magical powers. Nov. 6, 2001. (17 years old)

I've gotten into modes at certain points in my life where literally anything was possible. I would influence the environment and people's thoughts and actions through the intense amounts of my energy. There have been times when I've been clairvoyant. I think that a lot of people have had experiences like that.

My power or energy is the strongest, most powerful, most magical thing I own as of yet.

This power/energy can make me unstoppable in sports if it is turned on. It allows me to create brilliant works in very short amounts of time. It can draw people to me. It can scare the hell out of people as well.

When I was younger, I didn't know how to control this power and it got me in trouble. I have a lot more control of it now, though I'm not sure that I'm completely in control of it. I'm sure that it hasn't reached its maximum potential yet. This power keeps me warm, literally. I think it's what makes me so hot blooded. I think Dad has the same sort of power, only it's more relaxed and so easier to control as it isn't so intense.

This piece so well describes this seventeen year old. The words that jump out at me now are "magical," "brilliant" and "intense." He often did "scare the hell out of me" as I tried to counter his intensity with my own. To describe these embarrassing moments would not do justice to the all-pervading love that filled our hearts even during rough times.

It is clear that Dan recognized the intensity of his own energy, and that he had discovered how to control its expression. He was right in the sense, that as a little fellow, he didn't seem to care how or where he was expressing it, and in public it was often hard for me to quell his outbursts and restore equanimity in order to assuage embarrassment. Because he was a kid, it was easier to excuse. However, it helped me realize I had to learn to deal with my own emotions as much as his.

I recognized in hindsight these episodes of challenging behavior were strenuous but expansive exercises for me, "boot camp" if you will, designed to steadily build my own inner strength for the bigger challenges yet to come. Opportunities sometimes come in unexpected ways.

Chapter 8:

Getting Assistance From Intuitives

When my five-year-old daughter, three years Dan's junior, was diagnosed with her Whilm's tumor, I visited an intuitive reader to secure the notion that I had not caused this disease. Even if it were a past life issue that came through my energy, I would have been very disheartened.

The story revealed was that she was working off a past "arrow" that went through her kidney. Lifetimes ago, the end of this Native American princess's life, had been a fate that was apparently meant for her medicine man father. In this current lifetime she was to survive the loss of a kidney. That word "survive" was important for my well-being. The positive information that came through this past life intuitive read was that, while she was dying, her father gifted her with healing energy that she would be using in future life times.

As it has come to be in our present life together, that is the case. She chooses to assist Native Americans and the Earth energy to enliven the healing processes. With two master's degrees, one in

Environmental Law, the other in Intercultural Communications, you might tag her as an intellect. However, her presence is one of a beautiful, divine feminine energy that celebrates ceremony and heart connection.

Earlier helpers

Bringing in "helpers" to learn about past influences came earlier when Deborah was still in-utero. In 1986, we moved off the campus of our local university where my husband taught business courses, while I lived and worked as a student. I had come to Iowa from Connecticut six years earlier to be in a large group of Transcendental Meditators. My goals were to help establish peace on the planet, complete a Master's Degree, and find a husband. I have to say, that the last two goals were accomplished, while World Peace seems to still be on the horizon. As an optimist, I have the consoling belief that humanity will survive and flourish.

In the throes of moving off campus and well into my second pregnancy, I had to pull harder than I would have wanted on my two-and-half-year-old son's hand, forcing him off the couch so the movers could do their job. He really didn't want to cooperate for some reason and let it be known with his stubborn behavior.

We did move into our first home, and in our thirty plus years here, have made somewhat of an "estate" with all our fixings up. As an aside, I overheard a woman attending our Memorial service years later mention to her husband how spiritually sublime the area felt. Her comment was, "See what happens when you live for a long time in one place." Maybe that comment is true, but with all the attention from clearings, a space imbued with years of meditating energy, transformational healing sessions and workshops, it is no wonder. I assume it just takes a sensitive being to know one.

When we first entered our new house in 1986, we were greeted by a stuffed turkey and a gun closet. The feeling of "entities" infiltrated the house, and we were guided to do a "clearing" of unwanted energies before moving in.

Shortly after the move, and blessed to hold a new baby girl, I was challenged to hold the energetic space for our young son. With cries of fear, he was expressing an angst that he was being physically touched at night in bed by some unknown, perhaps, malevolent being. Was it his imagination, or was this trauma real? My approach was just one of verbal consoling. But, these events continued. What to do?

So, again, we sought a helper who came to his rescue. Our intuitive healer friend told little Daniel about an off-planet "Indian Chief" that was to become his personal guide. Then, this intuitive friend along with four-year-old Daniel and his special "Indian Chief" walked and cleared the land. How this happened I'll never really know. But the story is that our property in the back was apparently holding two hundred bound souls from a past violent massacre, and together they freed these spirits so they could go back to the Light, whatever that meant. Daniel then seemed to be released from the physical goading of some being who was looking for this freedom.

In addition, Daniel and his intuitive helper, cleared four hundred acres of land next to our property, and soon enough, the poisonously spiked Hawthorne trees miraculously vanished. Hmmm.

More assistance

School wasn't much of a joy for Daniel. His kindergarten teacher thought there was something wrong with him because his small motor skills weren't up to par. I didn't worry much about it though. I mostly worried that he could hang on all afternoon since he still liked to take two-hour naps during that time. Somehow, no matter how hard I tried to convince the administration, I couldn't get him into a morning class. And, I had to deal with some bad behavior most days when I left him as he really didn't want to be away from home. I just needed time with my little girl and a reprieve without him for a couple of hours.

One of Daniel's challenges as a youngster was feeling ok going into certain buildings and confronting people holding negative energy. Apparently, he was empathic and sensitive to dark energies in places like museums and cellars, and he could feel others' pain in his own body. So, I took him to have some lessons on how to move people's energy and clear unwanted energies in his environment. He must have learned this well because later he seemed to have no compunction about stopping and talking to the homeless people and other beggars that asked for money and needed attention as we walked through New York City or Washington, D.C. while vacationing. I was just never sure whether they were really helpless, or just scammers. So I always kept walking.

The gift of meeting Kaitlin

Looking back, I realize how blessed Daniel and I were to be introduced to people who could help us out in our trials on the planet. One time, when together in our local bookstore, we enjoyed looking for material for a second grade school project. We were alone, and I noticed the attentive woman behind the service desk. I recognized her. "Hi, Deanna," I said, "do you remember me?" I had visited this intuitive in the past to shed some light on my life. Sweetly, with a heartfelt apology, she said she went by Kaitlin now, and didn't remember our former exchange. When I mentioned I had some questions about Daniel, she was totally on board. I could tell that she was fascinated and felt connected to this unusual young boy, and suggested I call her in a few days.

That I did, and they took a walk and talk in the woods, and became friends, right up until his leaving. I assume, knowing them, that they stay connected. Kaitlin, working here on the planet, and Dan, from the inter-dimensional realm, are not bound to any concept of distance.

Kaitlin's assistance continued off and on. She was a real God-send during Dan's Bar Mitzvah. After we took our family photos, I could see his grounded energy leaving, and wondered if he could go through with the spiritual role of "becoming a man" through this rite of passage. A wave of fear came through me, and I prayed to God, (glad to be in a religious hall) that this would all work out. I must have been heard, for the ritual went forward okay. I later learned that Kaitlin, sitting in the back row of the congregation, used her energy to keep him present and focused.

In a discussion with her, after Dan's exit from the planet, she reminded me of their first conversation and walk in the woods. She mentioned that there was so much wisdom and heart connection in their dialogue, and neither one had to open their mouth. So, I remembered that he was not only empathic, but telepathic. It made me wish I could have been a more sensitive mother to this amazing soul. My excuse was that I was just an ordinary earthling.

Chapter 9

Many Roles To Play

"All the world's a stage, and all the men and women merely players; they have their exits and their entrances. And one man in his time plays many parts."

— *William Shakespeare*

Dan and Shakespeare had this much in common.

Dan had a fascination with theater, performance and magic. His ability to create new realities began with childhood games created with his playmates, little men and women superhero figurines. I'd watch entire worlds appear through his many voices and quick-moving hands engaging his "men" on our coffee table.

When he was old enough to become his own character, he took part in local musicals, went to magic camp and film school in New York, and became the lead in the camp plays as a teen. The drama department was very popular at this summer spot of one thousand campers in upper state New York. Somehow, I never saw these plays live, only on video where he assumed the lead. "Charlie Brown's Christmas," "A Funny Thing Happened on the

Way to the Forum," and "How to Succeed in Business without Really Trying" are the ones I remember.

Dan agreed to be the lead star in magic performances at home, full stage shows that his Dad wrote, produced and directed two consecutive years when Daniel returned from Magic Camp in Long Island. "Elephant's Up My Sleeve," and "No Strings Attached" were a big hit in the community filled with entertaining scripts behind the magic and some audience participation. Dan was thirteen and fourteen and completely at ease in front of an audience.

Just before opening night of "No Strings Attached," Dan broke his arm, and I thought the play was doomed. But he came through nicely, cast and all with the opening line, "I always wanted to perform with a full cast." Even the 'dancing cane' went well, which was quite a beautiful thing to watch with or without a cast.

He was a real ham (not bad for a Jewish kid), and was particularly good delivering his lines. He loved becoming the different characters necessary to draw in the audience. The more intense and quirky the roles were, the more he liked them.

"Flowers for Algernon"

Once camp had something to offer his passion, Dan was completely agreeable to the idea of going. He made formal application to a music and theater camp in Michigan. He was turning thirteen that summer, and I remember taping a few minutes of his monologue from "Flowers for Algernon" as part of his camp application. The performance really pulled at my heart strings as Charlie, the main character, a mentally retarded young adult, talks in his simpleton ways about taking abuse and laughs from other adults around him. As the story goes, the magic of a surgical experiment worked to develop a genius intellect. It was the emotional catching up that ensued, with the intellectual advancement eventually wearing off. Charlie reverts to the simpleton he once was with the disease leading to his pre-mature death.

If this scene could transmute into a video clip here, I would enjoy showing it. The scene involved the retarded, confused Charlie that Dan emulated so well. The soliloquy is from the stage of Charlie's life when the scientist presents him with the tests prior to the "experiment." In some ways, I felt Dan's performance in this scene was superior to the exposition in the feature film. In any case, he drew in an immense compassionate response from me and apparently the camp staff. He was accepted.

I want to present some examples of Charlie's comments before, during and after his intellectual enhancement as the subject of this scientific experiment. There seems to be some parallel to Dan's life story, where he found it difficult to interpret and integrate his fast-growing experiences in consciousness.

Before: *Its easy to make frends if you let pepul laff at you.*

In process: *Only a short time ago, I learned that people laughed at me. Now I can see that unknowingly I joined them in laughing at myself. That hurts the most.*

Results: *I don't know what's worse: to not know what you are and be happy, or to become what you've always wanted to be, and feel alone.*

Later that summer, Fred went to see the Camp's theater presentation of "Number the Starts" for visitor's weekend. It was about how the Danes helped the Jews escape from the Nazis. Dan, the only Jew in the cast, played the Nazi soldier. Somehow, that was the intensity that our son enjoyed. He continued his passion later on when applying to the University of Wisconsin to begin his college days. He began as a theater major, but ended up transferring to the business department. He graduated with a business degree, eventually going on to law school. The practical nature of his life began to make sense to me. It did seem that he was going to be around for a while.

Ted's Film

Now at Maharishi University of Management majoring in business for his last two years of college, Dan opted to befriend those who were the artsy types. He himself dabbled in film as an actor though in minor roles at this point, and also as a rooky film maker. His last acting gig was as a demi-god in his friend's final film project for school.

The name of the film is "Kappa," a demonized nature spirit in traditional Japanese folklore. I asked his friend, Ted, to explain the film and its symbolism. Before answering my questions, Ted wanted to share the film's conceptions. He confessed that Dan, in his usual way of exciting change in people, was the inspiration for the script. According to a an intuitive reading from Dan, Ted had been trapped in a series of inter-dimensional realms during past lives. He was passed around from realm to realm for being different. Unsuccessful in his search to find a place he could finally belong, this idea never left this filmmaker, and he decided to transform this feeling of being trapped by executing this movie.

The plot: Releasing the Shackles of Inequality

The experimental film is about an outcast soul, the Kappa, who is locked out of any place he can call home. He finds an open portal, which leads to a realm of fire and water, ruled by a crocodile-headed Demiurge (played by Dan in costume). Clad in chains, this Demiurge has made the place a lifeless waste and spends his time burning hopes and dreams that his dead subjects have left behind.

Dan, the demi-god, masked and chained, was a traditional fiery being, struggling to remove his bondage. He represented the cruel judge, some sort of tyrant that sought to control the universe. Jared, his real-life friend, played the Kappa, the seeker, who crawls from universe to universe, from green flourishing meadows to hell-like, fiery abodes that defy description. Looking everywhere for guidance, the ideas of hope and dream fulfillment are lost in the fire of destruction.

Upon entering the Demiurge's realm, the Kappa is detected with suspicion. The Demiurge then sends his servant to destroy the interloper. Upon discovering that the intruder is harmless, this compassionate servant becomes Kappa's friend. As is predictable, the Demiurge is enraged when he learns of his servant's "betrayal" and lashes out at this servant. Recognizing the beast's emotional turbulent struggles, the new friends courageously release the chains from the Demiurge, only to reveal this wild demi-god's underlying vulnerability and sadness.

Freed from the demonic urge to control, the Demiurge realizes his need to find Truth. The three characters form a triple bond of equality, and together break all chains keeping them from their goal of Truth. They enter the portals of hope and dream in an aura of light with a silent message of,

> *We are all equals in our ability to find guidance. Spiritual guidance is available for everyone. We belong together as beings on the planet and elsewhere.*

The dedication

The film was being edited at the time Dan was buying the gun and was bringing in the energy to pull the trigger. Ted was unaware of the event, and the film was completed the same morning that Dan fired the bullet in a clapping thunderstorm. Needless to say, Ted was heartbroken, and added to the credits an "in memoriam."

The short film was shown with those of the other students that next week, and apparently many tears were shed. I didn't have the courage to watch it until July 29, which would have been Dan's twenty-sixth birthday. To my own surprise, I was totally okay seeing it, feeling nourished by his digital presence.

Chapter 10

Dan's Real Job

At the same time Dan worked a full-time job and pursued an online master's degree program in accounting, he had another job. This was his real job, as he determined it—an on-line spiritual mentor. Apparently when he came back from law school in California, he had "met" a German woman online who would help him sort out his thinking which seemed very confused at the time. From our side, we were not sure she could really help him out, but somehow that lead to other spiritual sites where he would check in.

Eventually, I learned the online chats became sentient knowledge and support from "dear Dan," sort of like a spiritual Dear Abby, I imagine. He was soon asked to be the mentor on a few forums. Since these conversations went on in the middle of the night, it caused me to worry and wonder if Dan got any sleep. Sleep and proper rest is a very important commodity to me, and it was clear that my value system didn't fit into his. I would wander into the music room, an addition adjacent to our house, at two or three in the morning to suggest that he get some sleep as there was work at nine a.m. for him. He would just smile and say,

"What's your issue, Mom?" And, so, this characterized the entire next year, my own sleep being compromised with concern for his well-being.

At some point, in exasperation, I suggested that he find a place of his own. Out of sight, out of mind, and sleep became high on my bucket list. When he felt ready financially, he rented a little house near his Dad's office. I breathed a sigh of relief that things were moving in a direction of normalcy. His Dad saw him every day, his lovely girlfriend continued her creative life of dance and spiritual growth with Dan, and I enjoyed having him over for lunch once a week.

Chapter 11

Dabbling In The Dark Side

For all the sentient knowledge that Dan shared with friends and clients, inspiring others for their evolutionary path, including me, this was the part of Dan that I wish I didn't have to address. However, to be fair, the "dark side" was an aspect of his personality, and in some measure, important for his creativity. I think it is best described through his music, what he liked to listen to as well as emulate in his performances.

My stance

In my enthusiasm for honoring his talents, I was invited one afternoon to his living room music studio. He rarely wanted me to come to his little house. I assumed it was because my mothering instincts would come out, and I'd start to clean, or organize, or want to help in some way. This was not ok with him. Now, I imagine, maybe he thought that I might detect a negative energy that he was playing around with. And, of course, I would have had something to say about it.

I then had to agree to just see him at our house for a weekly lunch, and take walks with him in the woods. But, this day, I was actually invited, and my internal enthusiasm was overflowing with a happiness that a mother feels when her offspring wants to share his or her creativity. The two hours were interesting and satisfying as he showed me how he layered his music with guitar, keyboard, and singing voiceovers. When I asked him to play some of his original music, I could feel his delight, and I was surprised at how much he had written.

I had never explored who Dan's musical influencers were, who he listened to, or even what he played at open mics until this book was being written. When I asked one of his music buddies for a list of groups he was attracted to, I became disenchanted. I listened to just enough of these picks to feel an ominous energetic buzz in my body. Hearing some of these groups rattled my comfort cage. "How could I have a son that was attracted to this ……?" But I have to admit, the connections make sense to me.

I am not encouraging you to look them up, but I feel an obligation to share a few of them. They include the Magnetic Fields band, with its tongue-in-cheek humor and black lyrics, Smashing Pumpkins with the song 'Bullet with Butterfly Wings' from the album "Mellon Collie and the Infinite Sadness," and the comedic rock duo, Tenacious D, where song lyrics include 'fueled by Satan.' These groups sold millions of records, so I guess Dan was not alone in his appreciation.

I knew Dan brought in the dark side (whatever that really means), in order to take his life. In one of my letters to him the days immediately after he left, I wrote, "I do appreciate never having to experience the dark side ever." And, in that same note, "The fact that you are so happy you came to have an earthly experience warms my heart. I am thrilled to have hosted you for this long. I am so pleased you are able to be in a place where you can be in your true power. You are wonderful to be helping us all. I really feel you deeply. Love you."

It is clear that I did my best to avoid having to even think about, what I consider, the creepy side of him.

The saving grace for me is that in spite of his desire to listen to and play this 'dark' music, whenever he would play and sing for me or put together a CD of songs for me, I was entertained with the Beatles and other 60's music that I grew up with and resonate with. It was Bob Dylan's "Knocking On Heaven's Door," sweet sounding, yet still ominously predictive of his desire to move on, that brought me to tears for quite a while after he was gone.

The intensity of the music he played and listened to must have reverberated in his soul, but it appears that it was just another one of his distractions while in a physical body.

Chapter 12

Dan's Evolution
of Thought and Being

Feeling trapped: the impetus to move forward

Dan's free writing that I never read during the days of their creation, gave me the knowledge of what was really going on inside of him. I am reluctant to share some pieces because of their harsh language, and because of how soft he had become and of who he is now. It wouldn't seem appropriate. But, it was clear that he had thought about taking his life in the manner he chose many years before the fateful day.

October 30 and 31, 2001
(senior year in high school)

I remember when life was simple. I remember when I didn't stop to think about where my life was going, when life was fun, like a game or a party. I remember when life was worth living. I hope and assume that it will be that way again. I remember the future when evolution takes hold and goes. It's up to me to change NOW. For tomorrow will never come. There's no right, no wrong how to be, only a freaking bullet to the head. Would I do it? Sometimes I wonder.

Boy, I'm glad I didn't read this then. I assume his high school teacher who had given the assignment took it with a grain of salt.

In his writing, he would ruminate when he was away from home, for instance during his time at the DC National Leadership Conference, at summer camp as lead in the play productions, places where he felt more at home than at home with his family and schoolmates. A comment in the school free writing assignment is, *I need to get away from it all, but don't know how to. I don't know it is possible. If there even is a way. I might be trapped.*

In another writing the next day, he was to choose something or someone he liked, disliked and felt neutral about. He used me as the subject of his assignment. Had I read this while he was still around, I might have taken his thoughts seriously enough to try to change my own behavior. I'm sure I would have felt stupid, angry, and a bit defensive as were my customary responses. And I would have also realized that I had no choice but to transform these undesirable reactions in order to secure our relationship and enhance my own evolution.

As it turned out, I did feel a little remorse when I read his essay, when it was too late to do anything about it. Now, the feeling is neutral because there is nothing I can do about his thoughts so many years ago. I don't hold on to blaming myself or sustain guilt from my former, however imperfect, behaviors. He wouldn't want that anyway.

I'll paraphrase his writing now. What he liked about me was

that I was sweet and nice, and that I was a gifted and talented healer. He felt lucky to be taken care of by this type of mom. What he didn't like was that I was not always emotionally balanced and, therefore, he couldn't depend on getting close to me. And, that I took a lot for granted.

I personally hope some of my behavior and his feelings changed over the next few years. I think so, as I started to look more closely at who I was and how I might be able to change.

Although he felt I was too micromanaging, especially about laying off the computer games, cleaning his room, and doing his meditation, he did what he wanted anyway. As you might imagine, the more we get into people's faces, the less they want to cooperate. Enough said. I take this now as sort of a normal response from a teen, but, of course, wish I had been easier, displaying a less demanding tone of voice.

In the end, he concludes that:

Growth is about getting to the point where you can no longer live with confining boundaries. You'll have to let go, or else you may actually end up killing yourself. I don't recommend the latter course because you'll simply have to come back and do it again. It will probably be much more difficult the second time around.

I like that he gets this, but at some point, he must have felt that he never really had to come back because he never had to be here in the first place. So much was shared about this by those who could seemingly check in with his soul after he left. I'll leave this belief up to you to digest, or not, but it somehow rings true to me.

At least he never recommended leaving the planet as a way out of difficulties to those he mentored.

The last piece that I will share here is his spiritual experience and understanding that took him to a place of coming to "grips" with who he was in the body. Some people call it awakening, but to me, like enlightenment, the terminology is never clear cut.

Recognizing Nature Support and Evolution

I breathe out a sigh of relief in sharing the next piece of Dan's writing. It's a place of recognition, trust, and choice.

> *Nature/Life does things FOR you, not TO you, and what life gives you is always exactly the next thing that you need to help you grow. The result is greater happiness. There are only two questions. When will nature give you what you need when you are ready to receive it, and how often are you doomed to repeat the same lesson over and over?*

He spends the rest of the essay talking about these queries. He concludes that the deeper the lesson, the more patient Nature tends to be with you. The more often Nature has to ask you to learn the lesson, the less patient Nature will be.

As his mom, I feel that maybe I was given the role of this Nature that he talks about, nagging him onward. He does seem to agree with this.

> *Life is the ultimate understanding parent, but sometimes that may mean tough love. We like to blame outside circumstances for our misery, but that is just childish and highly inaccurate. I've seen over and over again how people set them-*

selves up for failure, misery, and all sorts of suffering simply because they are not listening to Nature and being open to what the Universe is trying to offer them.

And then he goes on to explain that it is easy to listen, and if there isn't obvious clarity, we just have to ask for it. He also mentions that negative and uncomfortable emotions are not the real YOU, and until one lets go of identifying with one's emotions, they will not leave. One of his clients who was able to make the transformation and let go of his anger remarked, "Wow, it's gone and I'm still here." Dan's whole method of emotional healing that he learned for himself and was able to impart to others was: accept the feelings, but don't define yourself by them.

Discovering Himself: Connecting to the Divine

The following words may not be clear to those who haven't had the experiences Dan attempts to describe below. Continually moving into living elevated spiritual realities, he needed to figure out how his physicality could remain here, on the planet, at the same time he was experiencing Divine perception. Although he may have been educated about the process of growth into higher states of consciousness, moving into the reality is an integration process that is not necessarily easy.

Dan jotted down a list of his progression in consciousness. I'm not sure of the timing, but my best guesstimate is that it was sometime in the fall of 2007. In the mention of a higher level of unified consciousness, he is speaking from his experience.

1. *I experience the enjoyment of God.*
2. *God disappears, only to realize that the perspective has*

merely shifted and I am looking through God's eyes. Everything is radiant with God's light which is coming from me and is not different from me.

3. *I am Brahman, the Absolute Creator of the universe. That cosmic body is MY Body.*

4. *Brahman, my Cosmic Body, is the Absolute observing the totality.*

5. *I, as Brahman, enter back into the Relative as it all comes back churning into life.*

6. *My Cosmic Body, in the Absolute viewing all of creation, is the same body as my physical functioning body. The Absolute unchanging field of life has moved into Relative life and takes on concrete form. It's not flashy, just simple, and SO peaceful.*

Accepting his Purpose

He explains that the results of all of this expansion and integration is a process that goes on indefinitely. The way he expresses it is an acceptance and celebration of who he is in the present moment, who he has become and is still becoming, and the purpose of his life.

I've finally accepted that all of my emotions are completely fine, so that I can meet people at whatever place they are. I can appreciate their emotional state without being overshadowed.

This is a very good place for an empathic individual to be, for sure. One of the most difficult challenges for empaths is to find a way to set personal boundaries and discriminate between their own emotions and those of others. The eventual gift for Dan, once he had figured this out, is that he could experience others' emotions and not be overshadowed by their feelings. That way he could help them heal. In my case, I feel fortunate to be able to help others without having to experience their emotions in my own body. Otherwise, I would have to figure it out, as he and others with empathic natures do.

Dan wrote,

I understand the purpose of being in a relative state here on the planet. There is nowhere else to be and this is the most concrete way the cosmic body can be experienced. Wow. How nice. Finally, the two have met and the Absolute and the Relative are now the same thing. And, I can experience both while being in my body.

As I have come to understand the levels of the growth of consciousness, once the unification of the unchanging, underlying nature of life is permanently established, the Unity of all of life is an on-going, permanent experience. As one loses identification with the small self, the ego, all of life is experienced from a greater totality. Life's bigger purpose unfolds.

I've finally accepted my path helping people spiritually while I work as an accountant. I have accepted being spiritually "out there" and whatever I need will come easily and effortlessly as time goes on. I am finally beginning to trust myself.

These were the topics that Dan would talk to me about a few weeks before he took it upon himself to be done with the physical. I enjoyed his expressions, but felt concerned about his concerns. He was beginning to question his ability to hold this powerful spiritual energy in his body and stay grounded. My fearful questioning about his staying was enlivened.

What is Normal?

There are other writings that continue to explain Dan's expanding consciousness. When he left law school, came home, and read in his room for four months, he learned more about who he was. One of his expressions was like the Rumi quote, "You are not a drop in the ocean. You are the ocean in an entire drop." Dan said, *"Even the cosmic value of Dan is just a drop in the ocean of what I am."*

Dan seemed to recognize, in the vastness of his own Being, Einstein's declarations that the observer is part of the equation. Objective proof and the unseen felt reality begin to merge.

Krishna (the most widely worshipped Hindu god) *is a Divine Being but is human as well. He simultaneously governs the universe and walks among it. The experience of this happening within my own being is for me every bit as visceral and solid as the feeling of the blood that runs through my veins. I cannot create my own Creation, but I am recognizing how everything I see is already creating the Creation. For me, this experience is as literal and concrete as I can possibly describe, as real as the experience of my physical body.*

If I am to ascribe any relative state of Being to myself, it is more like "normal" than any higher state attribution. I like the sound of normal. It silently speaks to the vast potential we have within ourselves just as we are.

This last statement gives tribute to the integration of higher consciousness while honoring the body. Although Dan recognized his physicality, he also knew through his own experience that his consciousness was able to blend this objective and subjective reality. With all this knowledge, it was difficult for me to understand why he didn't want to stay. This apparently had to become clarified for me when he chose to leave.

Once he felt his choice was obvious, Dan humbly admitted to me that he was a "light being," a kind of avatar that was not really connected to earthly life. He only slept about four hours a night for over a year by then, and I could not really understand how he managed to be "with it" while going to work, studying for a master's degree, and working with clients in person and online. He was becoming sweeter and softer, receding from the concrete reality of life as we know it here. Is that a prelude to becoming total "light?"

The Role of Spiritual Advisor: Using the gift of consciousness

During his growing manhood and realization of who he was, Dan's silence became very powerful. He was well loved and regarded at weekly Advaita (one of the classic Indian paths to spiritual realization) meetings where people came together to share their heightened experiences of consciousness. He didn't speak much, but his presence seemed necessary. I only went to the meeting once just to see what it was like. The spiritual support he lent to the group, even in his silence, was very apparent.

In addition to these weekly meetings, Dan, in his search for meaning here on the planet, had joined some spiritual forums on the web. Because of his questions and sentient responses to others, he was apparently asked to be the mentor on these sites. He seemed to agree (I only got this from hearsay), and when he left, there was some backlash from those he had connected with. "How could this possibly be?" was the heart wrenching experience for those that had relied on him.

He also had a few clients in town as well as those long distance on the phone, who seemed to feel soothed by his compassionate and useful advice. During the Memorial Service, one dear friend spoke of her beautiful and special connection with him this way, bringing tears of sweet memories to our eyes.

It seems that not everyone was that understanding and forgiving, but Nature spared me learning of these instances.

The only disparaging response that I had to deal with right away came from a message on Dan's cell phone, which we listened to soon after his departure. Apparently he had made an appointment with someone the day of, and, of course, he was not available. There was anger in her voice, and I had to call and tell her what had happened. No response came forth, and to this day, whenever I see her visiting in town, she can't look at me. Oh well. I did my part.

My grooming as a spiritual and inspirational coach came differently, and my learning is still meant to be solidly rooted here until such time that nature takes over and I am to return to my next home and the dust of the earth.

Normal Traits of the "Warrior-of-Light"

The term, "warrior-of-light" belongs to an article sent to me through Facebook. It is meant to serve as an inspiration for those having experiences of gaining spiritual awareness and of accepting certain feelings while playing one's part in the world.

Although the following traits rang true for Dan, he did leave. Even those who feel they are spiritually awakened to some degree and still hold some discomfort need not consider leaving.

The article, entitled "Things That Happen When You are An Awakened Soul on Earth," puts forth the following tenets:

1. *You feel as if you don't belong in this world and you get the urge to go "home."*

Even if this feeling is true as it was with Dan, his counsel would have been that it is important to find a way to work through the feeling in order to stay present on the planet.

2. *You become more compassionate. You are completely aware that healing comes from the heart.*

To exemplify this, Dan was able to communicate with animals and nature from a young age. He took a course on communication with animals, read books like "Kinship with All Life," by J. Allen Boone, and occasionally talked to the owners of pets who felt they needed to know what these speechless animals were thinking. Since most people didn't know Dan had this capability, it was kept private unless it leaked out.

A couple of times Dan was able to soothe the hearts of parents who had autistic children. He was able to help them understand what their child was thinking. A very heartwarming and tremendously healing experience came forth with a clear exchange of love beyond what words could convey.

3. *You just know things.*

You don't need words anymore. You need space and time to pray, contemplate and meditate. You are sensitive to overcrowded places and can easily be overwhelmed by other's energy and vibrations.

When Dan was quite young, he needed to learn how to function in certain environments and not be afraid or overwhelmed. Even going into a museum with old relics, some of which carried negative energies, alerted him to learn how to use his energy to protect himself. Since discovering that he was telepathic when he was nine, I began to understand him better. I was not able to read minds, so I encouraged him to not assume I knew what he was thinking.

4. *People always tell you about their problems. There is a fine thread of light that connects light warriors with others. Their heart is wide open and people feel safe to confess their secrets, confide their problems and share personal experiences. Light warriors are careful listeners who help others in time of difficulties by conveying the universal wisdom.*

The fact that he became a spiritual mentor online and in person attests to this quality. In a moving testimonial at his Memorial, a client and friend of Dan's actually revealed that she told him things that she never shared with anyone else, and felt he was more than a best friend.

5. *Light warriors are not afraid of death and dying. Death is nothing but a door that leads to another level of existence.*

The illusion of death as a finality is a belief that can be dispelled for those who carry any fear around it.

The final charge in this article is:

6. *As a warrior of light, your task is to keep your heart open, cultivate your conscious mind, and help others 'survive' the transition we're going through. It's not your job to change anybody. Just accept their choices and spread the Divine Light.*

And, so, the reality now is that Dan seems to be onboard to help others on the planet from an inter-dimensional place. He helps people survive in the midst of his need to have changed his own reality.

Chapter 13

Breaking Through "A Wall Of Infinity"

After a year of law school in California, Dan said he hit "a wall of infinity" and he couldn't go to class anymore. Nothing made sense to him to read, and he cloistered himself in his studio apartment high up in Russian Hill, San Francisco, ordering in pizza.

I was continuing to send him Bach Flower and homeopathic remedies in order to support his internal dilemmas, only to find later that he never opened one of them. My first suggestion after his news of isolation was that he see the school psychologist, which he did. Maybe she could help. When I called a few days later to find out what transpired, he said, "Oh, she likes me, and I'm teaching her a lot."

Not exactly the response I expected. I offered him to come home. "Really, it's ok."

He humbly agreed with a caveat. With a breath of relief from both sides, he did warn me that he would need to be in his room, and I would need to accept and respect his silence. He said that he would just be reading, coming down for lunch, and not speaking much. In other words, I was not to interfere with his internal reality, his thoughts, and his inner mission. Of course, I agreed without a blink, knowing that he would be under his mamma's wing on site.

Home again?

My heart was thrilled to receive him. He managed to sell his belongings, close out his San Francisco apartment lease and come home to the Midwest within a few days.

Days, weeks and months passed as Dan kept his promised silence. He would come down for lunch with a loving smile, no words, and climb the stairs to his room cave. Books, all of a spiritual nature, were devoured as I did see them pile up when I would guiltily peek into his room on occasion. I continued to worry in concern for his choice to remain a hermit in the house.

Yet, I continued to keep my agreement. He would show up each day for lunch without fail, and remain quietly in his room, day after day, week after week, and, month after month. Inside, I was kind of freaking out at the duration of this inner journey of his. Even though I had been on an intensified spiritual journey of my own around the same age as he was then, it was in the context of the TM Movement, on meditation courses, where hundreds of others took part in the same program. I personally could never imagine "going it alone."

By this time, Deborah was under the "protection" of Wheaton College in Massachusetts, my laissez-faire husband off to work each day, and I was left to ponder about Dan's eventual emergence from what seemed to be an indeterminate reprieve from life. One day, some four months later, I began to break my silence and test the waters. I suggested to Dan that he might consider working in his Dad's accounting firm part time. He did say he would. Inside I knew he felt an obligation to make some money and create some self-sufficiency.

My husband, easy with the natural flow of life, welcomed him as a budding junior accountant. I felt a new era of life was beginning. The following two years were interesting as Dan worked himself into a full-time position with the firm and nearly completed his on-line master's degree in accounting. With a lovely girlfriend at his side, the two of them created a healing, evolutionary bond. They continually worked on improving their relationship, and opened their hearts to help others with their challenges in life as spiritual counselors.

People in the community loved seeing Dan and his Dad strolling to lunch together, both expanded beings with huge hearts, always uplifting others in their wake, silently or otherwise. It was such a joy to me. My husband, nearly six feet tall, seems diminutive next to his pillar of a son. Made me smile.

Chapter 14

Dan's Writings

After Dan vacated the planet, we found writings from his on-line spiritual mentoring sessions in addition to the piles of papers from his closet at our home. With the information I gleaned from his thinking and experiences on our walk and talks, I had suggested that he might like to write a book. That was not on his agenda, so this book is as close as it gets.

He came up with a lot of ideas that may perplex those who are not thinking about their inner reality, their experiences in consciousness. His discussions were not meant for others to understand him, but rather for them to understand themselves. Once he understood his own relationship to God and the divine realm, he was able to help others do the same.

His format was always questions and answers. He told me that he would only give out necessary information if he were asked. I find it amusing as the teaching of my transformational healing process is a series of questions.

I do not want to belabor full client conversations that we found on the net, but I will include snippets of conversations we discovered. They became helpful for my own healing as I became clearer in my recognition of Dan's true nature. In this way, I guess you could say, he was there for me while being somewhere else, if this makes any sense.

The sections are unedited words that Dan wrote in response to clients' questions.

On Fear

The interesting thing is that fear can arise, and it's not a big deal. Fear is a perfectly safe feeling, and does not necessarily indicate any actual danger. On the most fundamental level, one cannot be hurt, and so there is an instinctual feeling of safety in there that cannot go away, even if fear (or pure terror) arises. So not only do those feelings arise less and less, but when they do, they are safe, and can even be totally comfortable.

This truth gave me some understanding of how he could possibly feel so much fear before he took his exit. He even mentioned it to me, and talked it out with many of his friends. I was told by intuitive friends, once the fear-based reality was a moot point for him, he was able to take fear from the planet. He apparently was commissioned to alleviate pain from those inhabiting the earth. Interesting concept since the fear of loss is dissipated with the loss itself.

On Wholeness

Perhaps each moment feels whole because it is. And THIS is what wholeness looks like right now. It can't look like any-

thing else in this moment. One way of talking about Enlight-
enment is that it is simply the acceptance of What Is.

I like the idea of wholeness being an all-time present reality. If that can be so, and if the totality of existence can be experienced in an integrated way, then enlightenment carries some kind of meaning to me. I'm not attached to the word itself, but it is a theme for people who have spiritual practices. The one thing I always want to say to "seekers," is that even though higher states of consciousness can be a practical reality, it isn't the end of experience. Rather, it seems to be a beginning, in which life can be lived from a place of comfort in complete acceptance and love.

On Sadness

Sadness is simply your heart reaching its edges and expanding to make more room. Let the sadness be there! Allowing the sadness, being with it, keeping it company and giving it the attention that it needs and deserves is the process by which the heart makes room for more of everything!

One piece of Dan's counsel is that any emotion is just fine, and that experiencing it to its fullest allows for completeness. It's like releasing the bad part of a negative emotion so it can be fully enjoyed. Then, in its full expression, something new can manifest. I imagine that just on the other side of sadness is happiness. In any case, I took this counsel to heart.

Also, in reading his definition, it became clear to me that there is a difference between the emotions of sadness and love. One can love someone in loss without feeling sad about it. And, that is not to minimize the importance of the grieving process, however it is meant to be experienced.

On Resistance

It's nearly impossible to see anything clearly that is being resisted, and the desire "to be done with it" is actually a subtle resistance to that process. The reasons those things hurt is because the resistance is still there. By feeling those resistances, those uncomfortable places until the whole situation resolves, then it's literally as if it was never there except sometimes as a faint memory, like it happened to someone else. It's again, like being okay with drowning so that one is no longer afraid of it. It doesn't help you get away from it, but it's away better than the stress of trying to avoid it.

I do have an issue with this drowning analogy. Somehow, we seem to want to survive at all costs, even at the cost of being afraid which he suggests causes resistance. However, I understand that it is of no use living in anticipatory fear, especially if the reality is simply made up. This fear would be born of a memory, past or present life, but not real in the moment, a useless carryover. As an unwarranted emotion, this fear is worth releasing.

I also notice with myself and with my clients that a neutral stance eradicates a former angst. For example, finding a life partner or succeeding in some way fulfills an unmet desire and therefore is no longer "unmet." An emotional charge behind any feeling of lack will disappear.

Surrender and feel through it

I think if you let yourself cry forever and fall apart and never be okay again, something wonderful will happen. That's my intuition, and it resonates with my being. Nothing will ever be the same again. In a very, very, good way. Just as long as the crying is the allowance of feeling the sadness and not an avoidance of it. It's the feeling that fixes it, not any particular response. That said, those responses, when natural, are good and important. I think you just may be on the brink of something absolutely wonderful.

I can understand that going through the "dark night of the soul," as it is often expressed, is sometimes necessary for rising to a much higher, lovelier state of existence. Here Dan seems to be encouraging someone to realize this potential. The inspiration is necessary. But then the work that he developed to release the emotions would be the next step, the DIS Emotional Release Process. That process is one of "not resisting" emotions, allowing them to surface and be felt fully in order to release them. I created my own version of this with the Empowerment Process called the Emotional Pathway Clearing. It does prove to very powerful and effective.

I assume that is what had to happen, no longer resisting some kind of "call," in order for him to leave this world though he never, and I mean never, suggested that anyone ever consider taking their own life. Although I keep harping on this message, I am adamant to get it across. Dan seemed to know, in his personal situation, that he would not have acquired any karma or negative impact from the act. Yet, this would not be true for most of us.

Also, from the tenor of his last sentence to the individual of counsel, "You may be on the brink of something wonderful," Dan seemed to have an unusual upbeat, positive and therapeutic tone. I guess that is why he was so loved and also why it was such a shock to so many when they discovered he was no longer there for them.

We found the following conversation from an online private Facebook post with someone whom I recently learned never met nor even spoke to Dan. The discussion, typical of the subject matter Dan churned around, was how divinity integrates with human life. The timing was a month before Dan transitioned. This fellow was kind enough to share the following with us.

"I was tempted to include a recorded online question and answer discussion just a month before Daniel transitioned. The subject discussed was Avatars, Gods, and Humans. However, the esoteric nature of the dialogue felt too confusing for me to investigate. One piece of content will give the flavor. Dan said, *The world isn't solid at all. I can put my consciousness right through it.*"

Stepping into Love

A rather poetic remembrance of Dan was posted on one of his mentoring chat sites. Apparently there was a lot of discussion back and forth with this particular gentleman. He did make the comment that he was surprised Dan's age was only twenty five. Maybe shocked is a better way to say it. This tribute began with the humorous comment:

"I don't know when he had the time to mentor. We hope he

wasn't doing our taxes… Dan was an evolutionary wind at my back. He shepherds me still. I read his words for hours today, and there is not a hint of fading power with which he effortlessly touches a life. Not that he wrote creatively, though he did, not that his love was angelic, though it was, not that he slogged for hours writing to helping me step into love which he did. It was the source that flowed through him that I'll never forget. For it's not the silence of missing him. Yet, I do cry and cry; his bell still tolls for me."

The Continuance of Love

This experience of someone loving Dan's presence, someone who never actually met him in person, is fascinating and soothing to me. It is the way I need to love now – to love the ethereal being we called Dan, my husband, my daughter, everyone I know, all of life on and off the planet. Since life on earth is short, and seems to be more so the older I get, I feel that I might as well practice "loving" from my heart, in thought and deed, with those here and now.

Most of us, if not all of us, have lost family members, and it seems to be the heart's memory that is most important. Our love is so much bigger than we probably even know, and so I want to be able to appreciate the heart's capability and use it all the time. There would be no divisions, wars, and negativity toward others at all if we honored such love.

As Dr. Jerry Jampolsky, a noted psychiatrist and author wrote, "Love knows that nothing is ever needed than more love."

Matthew Reifslager, who documented Divine Mother's messages in his 2009 Book, "The Wholeness," mentions that, "These conversations and experiences were clearly beyond the limited mental realm in which I had been used to operating, but at the same time felt deeply natural."

Chapter 15

Letting Go And Big Changes

One day Dan confided in me, "You can't imagine the fear I am carrying." I responded that I thought I could imagine.

Well, he was right, and I was wrong.

His sudden decision to leave the Office after the 2010 tax deadline was a time to investigate his purpose in life. I wasn't sure what this would lead to, or what he would discover. He ate well and seemed to take care of himself okay. We took our usual walks and talks and stayed pretty connected as he humbly revealed to me that he was an Avatar. His definition of this term, when I asked, was that he was simply a Light Being from another dimension. He explained to me that he remembered his life before he landed on this planet. I was unconcerned with this announcement, and didn't really care how he defined himself. There seemed to be no ego attached, and I knew he was special and didn't care how he saw himself. I actually thought to myself, "So kind of me to bring you in," though I didn't share these words.

This was not the first time he had made space for himself, and I was not expecting it to be four months long as he had carved out before he started work. I did begin to feel concerned though as he seemed to spend lots of time figuring out what to do next, and did not come to any concrete conclusions. His Dad would share his life's path and beliefs, describing the milestones and benefits of evolution while we were on the planet. Dan, however, dismissed this reasoning as short sighted, at least for himself.

In the next few weeks, Dan felt he needed to be more grounded in his efforts to use his energy effectively. I did not realize the extent of this need until I learned that he was receiving hugs from someone so that he could feel more solidly connected to the planet. He mentioned this to me, but I did not understand the enormity of what was actually going on. Of course, I felt this might be a good idea, but I did not inquire further.

My last hug, May 23, 2010

On the Sunday of Deborah's graduation party, Dan showed up early and left early.

I hugged my son as he was leaving the party. "Bye sweetheart." The words didn't feel right.

It wasn't the same full, luxurious hug I was accustomed to, my head gently pressing against his heart, a perfect fit for my height. Sweet, endearing and long, like an eternal wave of extended bliss. This one was shorter and felt incomplete. I could tell he was holding back as if he were afraid that I would keep him here by virtue of pure love.

Handing him some left-over goodies, he agreed to keep them in his freezer for another event coming up a couple of days later. My heart felt heavy, sinking into a subtle knowingness of a difficult path ahead.

My attention moved back to my guests and my girl, who was not feeling very well. Her ability to be sweetly present for those around her prevailed though, and our wedding anniversary took a back seat that day to the honoring of Deborah's accomplishments, and the unacknowledged fear lingering in the back of my mind.

Staying Grounded

Dan mentioned that someone was contributing to his well-being with hugs. When he told me that someone named Shiva Ma was helping him to stay grounded with hugs, I wrinkled my brow and wondered what this was about. Who was this Shiva Ma anyway? I guessed that he must be struggling to stay on the planet. Isn't that what being grounded meant? I didn't want to acknowledge that I could see his physiology becoming increasingly more transparent, and that I, his mom, was not the one that was helping him out. I did not want to believe any of this.

While writing this book, I decided to ask this beautiful "hugger" to share her experience.

Shiva Ma was a great blessing to Dan at a time when he was feeling the need to stay grounded. In her simplicity and innocence, she was able to support him in a way that held no agenda other than to love. I honestly wish that I could have fulfilled that role, but my worry and angst kept me from holding him so close without falling apart myself. Now, in his decision to go back to the Divine Mother, he was set free without any interference from family attachments.

Shiva Ma's Experience: More love

To recall an experience one needs to silence the mind and enter the HEART. As I call upon my heart to remember a beautiful soul named Dan, I surrender to simplicity.

I now take myself back to that morning when I was relaxing in my morning bath and feeling nurtured by the hot water.

This was my morning ritual, lying in the tub sometimes for hours, taking phone calls from my friends. Those dear souls who were troubled by this thing or that, needing support, understanding and love.

I was suddenly startled by a loud voice coming from my kitchen, which was on the first floor of my home.

"SHIVA MA! SOMEONE NEEDS YOU RIGHT NOW!"

I yelled who's there? I heard the voice say: "It's Eden."

Without hesitating for a second or asking: "Who needs me and why?" I jumped out of the tub grabbed my towel wrapped my wet hair in it, put on my bathrobe and ran downstairs.

Eden was standing in the kitchen alone so I asked: "What's going on?" She replied: "There's a young guy outside named Dan that needs to talk to you."

I went out into my yard and saw a very sad looking tall young man that looked like one of those beautiful beings from the movie "Avatar."

I slowly approached him and said: "Are you ok?"

He looked down at me with the eyes of despair and they melted my heart. I knew instantly what he needed. I said: "I think you need a hug!" At that he literally melted into my arms and buried his head in my chest. His 6'4 body bent over so that he was able to lean his head into my heart.

I felt like I was holding a tiny child that was helpless and fragile. I was deeply infused with a mother's love, as if I was holding my own son. I could feel his pain, his aching troubled heart. Tears flowed down my face as I continued to hold him. I knew that I couldn't let go, I felt that I needed to embrace him as long as he held me. The weight of his body slowly began to feel very heavy, but I didn't dare shift my weight or move in any way, knowing that if I did he would lose the surrendered feeling of safety and love that I was silently showering on him.

I thought to myself I'm not going to move until he lets go of me. I have no idea how long we stood there, it seemed on some level like an eternity. A soul searching for the comfort of his Universal Mother. The Mother who had the ability to take away all of his heartache and pain. I knew I had to be that mother for him at that moment, so I continued to hold him and let the waves of his sadness pass through me. The thought would come now and then can I hold up his weight any longer? He's getting so heavy, but I knew I couldn't let go until he felt revived, restored, renewed. How much time passed I'll never know, but after what seemed like forever he let go. He stood up and looked down at me with beaming light filled eyes full of Divine Love.

There was no need to ask him what his problem had been, no need to discuss anything. He felt better, it was obvious from the smile on his face.

I suggested that if he wanted me to help him that I would be happy to work with him, if he promised to come each day for a hug.

That was my recommendation, a hug every day for at least a week. No talking, no analyzing, no seeking any solutions just a simple loving hug daily.

He was so tickled by this idea and easily agreed. So began the hugging sessions. Each day he came and we hugged without talking. It was such a fulfilling experience for me to see how everyday he became happier, more at ease, more confidant. I looked forward to that hug each day. I loved feeling him against my chest like a baby, knowing that he was getting happier each day.

I am so grateful that I was able to share those precious moments with Dan. I love you, Dan.

Chapter 16

The Time Came

During a hugging break when Shiva Ma was busy hosting a visit from her mom, Dan mentioned that he had agreed to be "on the land" with a close friend. His plan was to work outside all day so he could stay connected to the Earth. When I asked how it went, he said "fine," but that it didn't change anything. So I, along with his friend, encouraged him to try again, but apparently, no coaxing would make the difference. My last words were, "Please stay in touch, you know how I worry." No answer came forth.

I had been trying to get in touch with Dan all day Tuesday. The few words we spoke Monday night remained in my thoughts. Being with his friend on the land was wonderful, but nothing had changed. Still no answer on Tuesday.

At lunch on Wednesday, I was eating at a local café with a friend to celebrate the completion of her medical program. She reminded me later that I spoke mostly about my worry and concern about Dan. When she suggested we go over to his place, I said I really wanted to, but he did not like me to just show up, so I would give it another day. That night we had sixty-five people over to the house, welcoming a new friend to town. Dan never showed up with the left-overs from Deb's party. He always kept his word. I put the concern on hold until after the party.

Once the guests departed, my anxiety became evident again. I called one of Dan's close friends to check in on him. He did answer the 11 p.m. call and mentioned that he was busy editing a film for school. He promised that if he finished in time, he would check in on him. That never happened.

The Discovery

Thursday morning came, and I couldn't settle in meditation. In a demanding voice to Fred, I insisted that we must go to Dan's place, admitting that I was afraid. Fred continued with his meditation mumbling that there was no hurry, he would probably still be sleeping any way. I could not contain the anxiety I felt in my body which made me literally jump out of my chair where I was meditating. In a fit of actual terror, I began speaking very directly and loudly that someone had to go to Dan's then and there, and that he had to go because I was too afraid. Didn't he get it?!

Hearing the commotion, Deborah came in, and with compassion and clarity in her voice, she noted that she was not afraid and would go over to his place. I gave her a huge hug hardly believing I could not take the responsibility to sooth my own ominous fear. She left, and I began to feel increasingly uneasy, overtaken by impatience and anger that I could not seem to do anything about. And, to top it off, Fred was not moving as he dove deeply into his blissful state.

Without another word, without any more waiting, I threw on my sneakers, and ran down our road as fast as I could, tears streaming down my face, holding in my desire to scream in order to relieve the tension. I was angry, angry that my husband would not support my immediate need to feel safe and know our son was okay.

I continued running, my emotions beginning to settle with my increased breathing as I reached the county park ten minutes later.

Upon entering the park, something unusual and extraordinary happened. Never before or since have I experienced such a world of Divine Presence and Light. The description is really beyond words, but I remember floating through the rays of sunlight, undaunted by any fear, guilt, or worries. All concerns just fell off like water rolling off my body as I emerged from the depths of a deep, dark ocean.

I didn't question this honorary expansiveness and walked in a Heavenly realm of beauty.   The plants exuded their sweet smells, the birds and insects opened into a grand, universal chorus, and the ground animals felt nourished as did I with a warm sun proudly beaming in a perfectly blue sky. I followed my usual path, and kept opening my heart to the universe. The onset of infinity broke forth, and I enjoyed thinking about my son in its midst. Time and dimension had no place. I kept walking, smiling, continuing in my blissful stance.

The only thoughts that came to me were ones that I now consider clairsentient, a knowingness that was not yet confirmed. As I crossed through the camp grounds, my mind came back into my body. I was thinking now, in more practical terms, "I wonder how much it would cost to build a third park cabin in honor of Daniel?" The two structures now standing in a primeval forest setting held a wide open, welcoming space in between them as if there were a need to fill it. I peered inside the windows, calculating how much it would cost to build a cabin like this….just like this, in memoriam to my son. Oh my, such a beautiful thought, to carry him on like this. For a moment I hesitated. "What am I thinking?" But, oh, it felt so right. My eyes filled with tears in some kind of gratitude that I didn't really understand.

As I left the park, I began to think about getting home, to discover what Deborah had met in her loving kindness to go to Dan's house…..and then I saw Fred's car racing down to meet me, hand on horn, intensity on his face…and I immediately knew….

Chapter 17

Forming A New Union

What happens to a family of four when it suddenly becomes a family of three? I wailed to my husband, "You don't have a son anymore." He did his best to console me with sweet assurance that Dan will always be there, held dearly in his heart. Although I felt reassured at his stalwart acceptance, a soul who has the ability to integrate quickly on many levels, I personally felt that I was gypped. How could this gap possibly be filled? Is it possible for a torn heart to mend? How the truth hurt.

Even though our house is good size, the three of us felt to stop at the top of the stairway in a huddle of grief and remembrance. Were we on our way to heaven, only to be halted in our tracks when the stair's landing appeared? We bonded together and shared for a couple of hours, just being there for each other in some spoken and unspoken way.

It was Thursday, I remembered as my mind came back to the present. I wanted to have the "celebration" of Dan's life on the following Monday, which was Memorial Day for the entire country! I had to somehow write an obituary for the local newspaper to be published the very next day. There would be no paper printed on

Saturday or Monday's holiday.

We reasoned as best we could manage in the immediacy of it all, that a Friday obituary notice would give the necessary three days to "sit Shiva," a traditional Jewish ritual, beginning that same evening.

Shaking with an upset of universal proportions, I sat in front of the computer, with my husband standing and directing me from behind. I focused really hard on my fingers as Fred dictated and I typed up an obituary for the next day's newspaper. The announcement was to also serve as an email to my friends and family members right away as I figured we could go with this hurried sequence of planning. How I wanted to honor that boy.

Once out with the information, we made important phone calls to my brother and sister-in-law. I asked my brother to pull to the side the road to receive the news. It was hard for him to hear, but he made a plane ticket, as did Fred's sister to be here Memorial Day for our "celebratory" event. The gift of family can never be minimized.

We were immediately barraged with emails of disbelief, full of condolences and heartfelt messages, many I didn't even read until days or weeks later. Those who didn't know Dan well, so many including relatives, were in complete shock, while close friends who knew of Dan's earthly dilemma, had to digest this reality with great remorse that there was nothing they could have done.

Our suggestion to contribute to a Memorial Fund in Dan's name was well honored, but not at the "expense" of our request to withhold sending flowers. The outpouring of love created a trail of footsteps, a well-known path for local flower shops. For the next few weeks our home smelled like a virtual botanical garden, blossoming into a perfume factory.

The cards and calls kept coming in almost as if they could replace the love that we seem to carry for a physical existence. How unbounded is a connection as we learn that love holds no concept of distance or even time, for that matter.

The Outpourings

Of course, even though we appreciated everyone's words of comfort and condolence, those that were the most precious to me were words that conveyed true understanding, true recognition of who Dan really was. Some came from those who had never met him in person. This gave me peace.

Here is an expression from a card that began as one of sympathy and ended as a note of thanks. Dan had intervened somehow.

"Dearest Janet,

I was about to write you about how sorry I was for your loss. A few minutes ago, I asked our friend how he did it. When she told me, in shock I asked how could he? Why?

Within that shock and the questions was programmed a golden key that opened a huge shift and gift. A shower of light came through me and the room. I knew it was from the beautiful Being that is your son…whom I never even met. I am in a state of surrounded GRACE. Thank you. Sending you many blessings and love."

On the following Mother's Day, twelve months later, Dan's sister wrote as if her brother were managing her pen.

Dear Mom,

Dan and I love you every much. I feel that he encourages me to write about abundant joy and energy for you everywhere. You have found the pathway to subtle grace.

She writes many more sweet thoughts and ends with this:

I know how much we miss Dan here with us. But I feel him and he likes to zoom around and shoot off energy in colors of hot pink and orange, like fireworks of celebration above us. We love you Mom, always honoring you near or far from home.

The truth for her was palpable in their continuing relationship, where distance never plays a part.

Chapter 18

The Cremation

Saying any kind of permanent "goodbye" must be a fantasy. I am not sure of the concept of goodbye when the heart is never released of connection, but rather resurrected anew. The day when the body is wheeled into an oven, when consuming flames of fire render the earthly form to ashes, is not an expression of finality by any means.

Fred, Deb and I were ushered into a blindingly lit garage, scrubbed pristine like a resort spa. The chairs awaiting us directly faced a large refrigerator. It took me a few moments to collect my senses from all this stimulation, hardly an atmosphere for this deeply solemn occasion.

I'm not sure what prompted my heart to pour out inspirational words, but my voice spilled out a wonderful sermon to a handful of close friends who stood with silent, loving energy. It carried on over the deafening intermittent phone blasts, bright light and veil of tears.

Recognizing that we were in a semi-circle surrounding an enormous refrigerator, it dawned on me that Dan's lifeless body was before me. It was right in front of my eyes, masked only by the large metal door. I asked the undertaker in attendance which direction Dan's head would be. As it was facing me, toward the door, I placed my hands on the spot where I thought he lay. My heart was pounding with the energy of love that I had only experienced during his birth. I could barely contain my own energy as I just blessed him. The love poured out, overflowing over itself.

Sitting down again, Hilary, his long-time girlfriend, now an "ex," appeared in due time, and we all closed our eyes amongst the hubbub to settle in meditation. In short order, I witnessed, or rather felt, "yes, it must have been the ascension." Dan rose out of his physical body and "flew" to his freedom, satisfied that we were all on board to wish him a pleasant journey. He had broken through the "wall of infinity" to the place he had so longed for.

Ceremony for the Departed

The next moment, a door swung open with a mummy-like proxy body being wheeled in as if going into a surgical procedure. At the helm was Jennifer, our Vedic chanting queen. Trained in the Vedic rites around death and dying and the treatment of the body in preparation for cremation, she was on board for all of us. The event of a suicide was not the usual for her, and I could see that her own ruffled energy needed to settle down and center so she could proceed with this "pretend" cadaver. She created an effigy to serve as an energetic focal point for this ritual.

It was later that Jennifer told me about the preparation of the little effigy. On hearing of our desire to have her officiate the Vedic rites prior to cremation, she asked for divine guidance to receive help and direction. In many traditions, suicide is considered a sin of great magnitude, a violation against the sanctity of an incarnated life. Usually the body is cremated without rites. As Jennifer had never done rites for someone who had taken their life, she told us that she prayed for mercy and help for Daniel. Immediately an exquisitely intense energy "arrived" to guide her. (Sometimes, I think it was Dan himself who compassionately came through to support his own transition.)

The information and directions she received was a highly charged spiritual experience for her. She felt not only Daniel's presence, but an urgency about creating it in a very specific manner. Certain materials were to be used, certain prayers to be said to help mitigate the karma of the suicide. Even though Dan did not seem to have acquired or necessitated the release of karma, having a human body must mean that some type of karma exists.

Jennifer described herself feeling like a puppet being moved around to gather and create the form. All the materials needed were natural as she crafted a small human-like figure covered in white cloth. During the preparation, she completed a Vedic body ritual with chanting, washing, anointing and wrapping the form before bringing the effigy to the crematorium. I wish, in some ways, that I'd been present to experience the energetic beauty of this preparation.

Jennifer explained to us that there are specific rituals in all traditions of Truth preparing for the release of the physical body and elevation of the soul into the Life Eternal. Although such ceremonies are often administered by a celebrant, the actual ritual is done by the collective of the loving family and friends. The rituals represent love in action to uplift, align, inform and heal all who are participating. In Jennifer's words:

The cremation ceremony itself was loaded with the palpable and natural grief of the many people attending...especially among Daniel's young friends. His parents were in another state...of grace and/or shock...and not in a place of struggle as so many others were. I felt the impact of these feelings as well as my own around Dan's sudden, violent departure. Fortunately, I felt my sensibilities fortified as I engaged in the ritual. As I stabilized, I was able to assume the task with a spiritual focus...to prepare, honor and release the natural elements of the body, now an 'empty temple' before them.

The ceremony for releasing the five elements having been completed, Daniel's effigy body was ready for his send-off by the group.

What followed proved to be a tender and intimate experience for each participant. Permission and space seemed to be given for the shedding of tears and shared love. The tone of the event continued to build into a tsunami of love for Daniel as we lay flowers around this precious non-being, our hearts flowing to the Divine Daniel.

Although it was evident that we seemed to be honoring a surrogate body, as it was almost a foot shorter than Dan's stature, the effigy had become Daniel's form for everyone. Those participating shared their sadness, feeling grateful to be participating in this compassionate ritual. This seeming surreal event brought hope that proved helpful for their own healing in the wake of offering a smooth transition for Daniel.

Once this ceremony came to an end, my husband, at the helm,

pushed the effigy and Dan's physical body into the giant oven, and our mission was completed. The fire, representing the release of the five elements back to nature, resolved any remaining connections to a physical vehicle. The rush of power was magnificent and readily felt as the body entered the crematory fire.

After the event, as Jennifer reported to me later, she went back to the Vedic literature to verify that nothing 'inappropriate' had occurred. She had some concern whether or not it would be traditionally okay to use an effigy as a substitute during the ceremony. To her amazement, she discovered the text with the confirming instruction. It was appropriate that an effigy be substituted when the physical body had been lost or badly damaged. Jennifer felt relief in the completion of what had been a very demanding task.

Chapter 19

Coming To Grips

In the Jewish tradition, there is a custom after burial that places loss and grief in the communal context of family and friends. The intention is that those who suffer a loss are comforted by this gathering.

In our case, the roles seemed to be reversed. That is, our role, my husband's, Dan's sister's, and mine, needed to be the comforting element to shocked and mournful beings, our family members and friends, and even unknowns. The numbers of attendees increased each evening from seventy-five, to one hundred twenty-five, to three hundred fifty as the three nights progressed. All these souls congregated even before the actual service on Memorial Day. Standing on our deck, day one, facing us as best as they could, friends needed to know. What happened? How could Dan, such a bright light and seemingly calming presence, have done this violent act? Was he depressed, full of unhappiness, crazy, or maybe even courageous, following his mission, as one friend later mentioned?

The outpouring of love escalated, bringing the community together for healing. Even those who did not know him came to make sense of it all and offer their healing influence. Beyond the emotional healing was an even more profound influence of spiritual upliftment for everyone present.

Sitting Shiva

Right from the first of the three days of sitting Shiva, such questions needed to be addressed as we felt obligated to sooth our bereft, heart-broken friends even in the midst of our own transformation.

Friday evening: The start of the Sabbath, which we didn't habitually celebrate formally, began with the lighting of candles. This time, the Hebrew prayers seemed to be directed toward Dan in the divine realm, somewhere off in the ether rather than to an amorphous being we would recognize as God.

Giving out the support necessary for those who came flowed easily, surrounded by so much love. For me, the evenings' memories melted into one another like an illusory dream. However, I do remember his former girlfriend's heart sharing. She helped me settle my own heart, my ability to accept the dramatic way Daniel chose to leave. She explained how she received his breaking up with her several weeks earlier. "I felt shafted when he left me several weeks ago." With a sort of confident knowingness, she spoke out. "But within five minutes, I recognized that I trusted him… more than anyone I'd ever trusted before, and that somehow, our paths were to divide and cross again in another way."

At that moment, a wave of absolution washed through me and my mind and emotions felt so much freer. It dispelled any doubt of the reality of who he was. It totally jibed with a message that came through to a friend shortly after Dan left. With this message, his unique reality was beginning to be revealed.

The message I am referring to was received a couple days after he left, by someone who really did not know him, and had never really met him. Surprised and taken aback by the information, it apparently took some goading from Daniel in his "new world" for her to share it. So she sent the email below. I later assured her how important it was to me and all of us that she followed his directive. That communication from me seemed to sooth her soul.

Dear Janet and Fred,

Since I heard of the passing of Daniel, my attention has been on him and both of you. As a consequence, Daniel's soul started communicating with me, and he was insistent that I share this message with you.

At first his soul was distraught by the pain his passing caused, you, your family, friends and community. Therefore, he wished to explain himself. After a day or two his soul became peaceful and very focused on your well- being, his sister, friends and community. What I am going to convey is very much in line with what both of you said tonight at your home.

His soul comes from a high angelic realm formed through union with the Divine. One of the missions of this realm is to help souls that are incarnated in different worlds. To better help those living on the planet Earth, his soul wanted to experience what it was like to be in a physical body. That is the main reason he came on Earth. He did not come to accomplish a mission, or evolve, just simply experience being a human being. To minimize the gap between his realm and planet Earth, he chose a high spiritual community and very spiritual parents.

He left, as he wanted to go back home. He was done with the experience. The way he chose to depart has no bearing on him or on his family. That is what he said when I thought, when someone commits suicide, there is some karma, etc. His answer was that it does not apply.

One cannot fathom a more challenging course of events to go through for mother and father to lose a child, but also it is one of the greatest opportunities to move to a cosmic level in order to understand it in a positive way. I am sure you do, based on what I heard tonight and how his soul is more peaceful.

Dan's soul is very much here, wishing to take care of everyone he has affected in one way or another. He is particularly concerned about the wellbeing of his sister. He said that it is important to support him in his decision to go. His time was up.

He said the reason that it is important to support his decision is that it brings peace to his soul. However, it is also important not to resist grieving as you integrate in the coming months. To view this challenging situation in a positive, cosmic light cultivates the establishment of unity consciousness. We are all One, always have been, always will be.

When I asked why he chose that particular way to depart, his answer was that his mother will know.

He also said that both of you were excellent parents and that there is nothing you could have done better. This will become more apparent in the future. The next few months will be of great integra-

tions and he will be there to help until it is accomplished.

This was important information for us, as there were some friends who thought we should have taken him to a psychiatrist and given him medication. Such a thought had crossed my mind a few years before, when he hit his "wall of infinity" in law school. The results were that he was the "therapist" and he seemed to have no intention of compromising this experience of infinite awareness. He just had to break through it in his way of conquering the Absolute!

Maybe I do know "why" he left the way he did, although I'm not a hundred percent certain. But here is my explanation. He wanted his departure to be his complete responsibility. He didn't want to end life in a car crash, as he would have destroyed the car we bought for him, a perfectly good vehicle, perhaps even putting another driver at risk. And, who knows, if he survived, he never wanted or needed to be disabled. In the same vein, he wouldn't have taken a drug overdose. He never ever took pills, drugs, alcohol, or any unnatural substance in his body. Perhaps he felt not to contaminate the "purity" of his Being, compromise any experience of higher consciousness. Taking something toxic into his body for the purpose of leaving might have backfired, creating the possibility of disabling his body. Becoming ill would not have worked. He basically was never sick. A rope or other method might cause physical suffering and he definitely wasn't into that.

It was easy to digest Dan's words as we heard over and over again in the coming days and weeks that he was not meant to be on Earth very long, or even needed to be here at all. The last part of the letter regarding his request to honor the way he left as it would give him peace seemed important for my well-being. It gave me a "reason" to be okay. Maybe this response from me is a bit overstated given such a giant loss, but it certainly helped my need to understand and accept the situation as much as I could at this delicate time.

Saturday Evening: My Surrender to Love and Acceptance

I wrote out what I wanted to say on the second day of sitting Shiva to share with our friends who came to learn more and support us and themselves from the devastation in our hearts. I felt this responsibility as they stood shocked in disbelief and concern for me and my family.

"Tonight I am here to share my love, the love of my son, the love of life, the love of the Divine.

It has been difficult for me to separate out the pain and the love, but they are separate. I breathe in the love, out the pain. The pain of not being able to do anything. The great sadness in loss.

But Dan would tell me to feel it fully, so deeply that it can heal itself. His message to others provided this patient, soft healing advice. Yet, he was only able to listen to his own heart for so long. The pain got stronger than the love he could garner from his family, friends, the universe, and ultimately, himself. Dan shared his feelings and love with me, Fred, and Deborah and his close friends. Almost daily, we were with him, though it be brief.

Monday night he told me he had given up. He appreciated all that he had been given, all that he was provided with to give others.

But now he had no incentive to go on. We talked to him about the possibility of medication. A dutiful son, he agreed. But, this was not his way. This was the last time he answered my phone calls.

I was always impressed how Dan was able to go it alone – work it out internally. He had so many ways to understand and heal, and sought council from a variety of sources to get to the next step: hundreds of books, online mentors, and internal spiritual guides, direct, deep conversations with close friends and with God. It was this ability I was hoping he could rely on Tuesday when he wouldn't pick up his phone.

It is because of Dan that I was pushed forward into my own gifts and was forced to share them with him and eventually my clients. He wouldn't let me resist my own growth – and he was the most powerful example and sometimes mentor for me. I have matured in my belief of inner transformation, and I am here for myself, for others, for God.

The sweetness and patience Dan had for me and others could melt statues. The anger and frustration he held was difficult to understand. His emotions were intense, but he witnessed the roller-coaster ride. He would always tell me he was fine, and that was mostly true.

I can only say that whatever time he had here was precious and well spent, and I have to accept how it ended. That place is hard to go, but Dan made a choice. I must honor it."

A few friends shared their hearts after we shared ours, and the atmosphere became more and more subtle, peaceful, and connected with a loving presence. There was a peace that grew fuller in my heart as the days moved on. And, to ease the pain, I spent a few minutes in the following days writing down my thoughts to him. Although I couldn't send the letters via air mail, or email, I knew they were received by ether mail.

Burning up the Grief

Sunday evening: Under a canopy in our yard with three hundred chairs, we joined the congregation overflowing with feelings of remorse, love, and sentient words. I watched the group energy, and I noticed throughout the evening that my attention was drawn to an out-of-town friend who held a knowing and satisfied aura of bliss and love. After the evening gathering, I asked if she would come to the porch and reveal what she was experiencing. I intuitively knew she had something important to share. As a sentient soul, intuitive healer, and family friend, she must have a part of the story that needed to reveal itself. (I often wonder if this meeting would have happened if I didn't make the overture.)

From nine until midnight, the evening took shape. Firstly, Reesa explained that when she received an email from a local friend who read Friday's obituary announcing Monday's Memorial Day event, she immediately checked in to support my energy. Being a Mom herself, and a personal friend, her heart felt the need to be there for me. But, apparently, Dan didn't arrive exactly where he thought he was going and needed immediate assistance to rejoin Mother Divine on the other side. He didn't want to waste time in any in-between state. So, she got an intercepting message from him, loud and clear.

She instantly took up the charge and called in her support system as she felt the intense, immediacy of the situation. Dan was given the chariot ride he was looking for. "Well done," I bowed with internal gratitude. I felt thankful that Dan "made it" to his destination.

The next event happened on the porch, and both Fred and Deborah joined us. We were guided to create an imaginary bonfire. The intent was for each of us to throw into the flames the grief, anger, confusion, and regrets that we, our family and friends, and even people we barely knew and didn't know would need to release. I was surprised how much we unloaded in the next hour or so as healing was clearly needed. So much sadness, disbelief, loss, heartache, fear, anger, and forgiveness came forth, one after the other, and more, and more. Throughout this ceremony, the love became more and more palpable.

Reesa suddenly interrupted our ceremony. "Did you see that?" What was this about? We tried to guess. Incredulously, she blurted, "You each have your own special Daniel behind each one of you." Apparently, he had divided into three separate beings that she could clearly see. And, a second later, Dan had divided into infinity. Yes, Dan had finally broken through "a wall of infinity" that he so intensely wanted while in his body.

A feeling came over me, similar to the one I had when he ascended just before the cremation. Yes, he made it. I began to feel some gratitude from accepting the possibility that he did make the right decision for himself.

Chapter 20

Why Dan Left The Way He Did

When Dan sent his message from the etheric realm to our friend, he indicated that I would know why he left the way he did. Why he left suddenly with a bullet to his head was a mystery to so many.

During the weeks before Dan made his transition, he sorrowfully admitted that he couldn't hold the dense vibration of the Earth in his subtle physiology any longer. So, in this sense, he had no choice. I say sorrowful because I think he felt my fear of losing him, and he really did feel badly for the grief he would cause for his family, friends, and the community that had raised and loved him.

It is clear to me that his leaving was planned ahead of time. He had paid all his bills, lived out the lease time in his rental house, finished out tax season at his Dad's office, and left his girlfriend a few weeks before. Since he apparently could not stay any longer, on a practical level his leaving had to be immediately effective and done with. He therefore followed his judgment and took a violent course of action. These were my words of explanation as I was challenged to make some sense out of his final performance.

In order to provide a greater level of understanding, I attempted to answer the "whys" that continued to surface. Not everyone could incorporate the reality into their belief system. What I shared with those who inquired and truthfully needed a deeper explanation was the information that I heard over and over by intuitive helpers, healers, and readers. The reality seemed to be that Dan had never been on the planet prior to this lifetime, and didn't really need to be here at all. His choice was to check it out and have a new adventure. Why not Earth then?

Dan's prior job in the non-physical

Occasionally, we would ask Dan what his memories were from his former life, off the planet. I remember him telling us the story of how he would help earth souls in transition, those leaving their body, to feel welcomed and guided. He would "take them by the hand" and lead them to the appropriate realm where they could continue to evolve and learn without the confinement of a physical body. He referred to this as having a job akin to a traffic cop. He felt that since he guided so many souls to incarnate on planet Earth, he should know more about it.

Perhaps meeting these former earth incarnates gave him the curiosity and impetus to try out an earthly life for himself. However, I personally don't remember agreeing to birth a "light being," but, apparently, I must have made that commitment in a pre-life contract.

Kaitlin's Sobering Message

In order to receive some immediate clarity and answer a few

questions, Fred and I arranged a long-distance phone call to the outback of Australia where Kaitlin now lives. In the conversation, she reminded us of that first walk she had with Dan, the young boy she had met in the bookstore. She mentioned that they had a marvelous communication during their walk when neither one of them had to open their mouths. I remembered that he was not only empathic, but telepathic and so could read my worrisome thoughts.

Her immediate response to the news and our queries was one of complete understanding without the need for remorse, sorrow, or even traditional consolation. She shared with us the following:

Daniel was not of this world. He came for a specific purpose. He made a tremendous sacrifice to come to this planet to serve. The only reason that he was able to stay as long as he did was because of the family he picked to support him in this service. He needed guidance and grounding from his family.

A note of recognition here. We had to put a large, heavy rock beneath his bed when he was little just to keep him feeling grounded. Now this rock, which I wheel-barreled out to our backyard cabin we felt to erect in his honor, is the first step into this abode of love.

It did not matter how he left and there will be no karmic repercussions for him. For a being of this kind there is no karma to be incurred here on Earth.

This was affirmed many times by others. An Eastern Astrologer friend, upon learning what had happened, offered to organize a ceremonial Yagya in India to ameliorate the effect of a suicide.

The information that we received via email after this performance was that the Yagya results ironically were meant for the healing of those remaining on the planet rather than this departed soul. Apparently, Dan didn't need such "help" and was karmically fine having made the decision to go "home."

Kaitlin continued:

For humans on Earth there would be different consequences. But Daniel was a different kind of being, one of a small number that comes to the Earth in any particular time.

He came to raise the vibrational system of the planet, and had raised his own vibrational system as much as his physiology would allow. He had fulfilled the service that he came for. The little dramas of life on Earth kept his attention but didn't serve him anymore. Nothing could have kept him here.

There was a part of me that felt some remorse that my husband and I couldn't have kept him here. We did try our best to explain, cajole, and beg. As you can imagine, bribery was not even a question in our thinking. Kaitlin's message gave me a confident realization that we, his family and friends, had done everything we could to keep him here. This knowing didn't snuff out the pain right away, but there is something about understanding through acknowledgement that helps in the healing process.

Words from Delores Cannon

Delores Cannon birthed a past life regression process that she developed over thirty years ago to help people heal and understand their life's purpose. She facilitated healings until her death in 2014, and reported her conversations with her clients' higher self in her "Convoluted Universe" book series. She would take her clients, through hypnosis, to a relevant past life in order to heal some issue arising in the present. In her section of 'Advanced Beings and Karma' in "Convoluted Universe," Book II, p.18, Delores shares her client's dialogue with her client's higher self which I have paraphrased.

She (her client) had previously worked behind the scenes to help others adjust to incarnate. She was never on Earth herself until this incarnation, and she will stay until her job is finished. She won't have to incarnate again. She will not accrue any karma while on the planet. She came to help others release their karma without getting caught up in it.

Kaitlin Answers more Questions

We had many more questions we needed answered after Dan's passing. Kaitlin blessed us with more understanding and insight. Our questions are written in bold.

Why couldn't Daniel finish this lifetime in a natural way, thinking that God would make the journey worthwhile?

His journey was not as a human being. He was simply an energy force that was offered to the planet, experiencing through a physical human body. He knew exactly what he was doing even though it didn't seem like it at times. The quest for him was not for peace. His quest was to process and release so much of the negative energy on the planet. We are reaching a critical mass with the number of light workers that are finally realizing that they don't have to do all of these processes — all they have to do is love. That's where the peace comes from. Arriving at a sense of peace was never his goal. But when it happened, he was gone. The day he remembered who he was, he could leave.

I have to admit, this explanation was eye opening and soothing to me at the same time. I do feel that he hung on longer than he would have liked. Maybe he developed an attachment to being here for those whom he loved and was mentoring. However, if he really had no choice, this information felt aligned with a closing comment from the Jyotish astrology reading ten years earlier. I was with Dan taking notes during the session and this is what I recorded. *"You will 'transcend' the gripping qualities of your own energy with a will of iron."*

Dan did manage to come to a peaceful understanding of who he was through the progression of expanded and integrated consciousness. And, according to Kaitlin, this was a completion and his message to exit. I imagine that the four months he hibernated and read in his room after leaving law school was a big boost to discovering who he was.

What was the source of Daniel's feeling of fear, anger, frustration, and anguish with life?

The key to understanding this whole situation is to remember that Daniel was not from this planet. He was not on the human evolutionary train. He was simply an impulse of energy that came to completely evolutionize the planet. Upon his birth, his job was complete. He was simply an outline that contained this energy and as time went on, the line started to blur. Because he was this light, this energy, he had an overwhelming empathic experience of this planet.

He felt everything. All of the anger, all of the fear, all of the negative energy on the planet he had to contend with. Any seemingly emotional fragility was because he was trying to process things for the planet. We couldn't help him because we were coming from the human level. He was transmuting all of these energies throughout the planet to serve its evolution. This seems very big. But it is the truth.

The Truth did seem big, and hard to swallow for some. I chose to accept this information, as it gave me peace and an understanding that helped heal myself and others.

There was one time that I did seem to be able to help with a leftover "project" after he ascended to his new home. During a solo walk in the woods a few weeks after he had left, I felt that I was being followed by a huge tail of grief. It was like a comet's tail that didn't seem to be coming out of me, but did engulf my energy. My impulse was to "fight against" the feeling or run away. Then I remembered Dan's counsel to just be with the emotion. I began to recognize that it was a left over energy in the environment that needed to be released.

With this knowledge and some energetic assistance, I was able to accept and process the emotion and allow it to release through my Being. A brief call on my cell phone to my psychic friend gave me the informational relief that I had done my job, and I could relax. The rest of the walk was calm and centered.

Kaitlin's explanation of his death

We have been so indoctrinated as to what is the best way to die, so any taking of life like that is going to resonate with us as a violent way to end a life. So, Daniel, being the dramatic personality that he was, chose that, and boy, hasn't it made everybody think about death and broken a lot of boundaries?"

It is interesting to me that many people really did understand who Dan was, and didn't take his suicide as an indication of a weakness. I liked the way Rich Archer expressed it at the Memorial Service. He talked about the act as a possible one of courage, to go home where he can be of greater service to the Earth, and to the inter-dimensional aspects that affect our planet. I am assuming that there are many Beings, on and off the planet, who are serving us all the time.

Why did Daniel leave when he did? Why could he not bring the fullness of Mother Divine to his experience and fulfill his quest?

The Earth cannot hold that energy at this time. The Earth cannot hold what Mother is. Mother is Mother Divine and Mother Earth, as well. But to bring that energy in at this time is not supportable. Daniel's physiology could not contain that energy, so he had no choice but to go back. His job was done; it was time to go home. Perfect peace.

I know there are people who have said that because he went out that way, he couldn't have been at peace. That is almost always true ninety-nine percent of the time. But it has absolutely nothing to do with Daniel. He did what was necessary, once he was able to remember.

Although I often wonder what he is up to, I treat him as I would if he were here and stay out of his business. I do remember the conversation with Reesa, who saw him divide into infinity while we were conversing with her on our porch one night of "sitting Shiva." I assume that it may not even be possible to keep track of someone who can be in so many places at once. I'm okay with that.

Chapter 21

Healing Begins

It is uncanny to me now that I was able to let go so quickly of Dan's physicality and go forward with my own and everyone else's healing. The event opened up an obvious truth for all of us. How can we grasp our condition as mortal beings and know that there is more to life than our life here? We are commissioned to learn as much as we can, contribute what we are willing and able to while we are here, and surrender to a divine will beyond our comprehension.

The day before the Memorial Service, as I was thinking about Dan and my role in these events, I wrote a talk that I never did deliver. It was to integrate my feelings even if they were never meant for others to hear. So I am speaking to an imaginary audience.

I wake up ready to receive. Ready to receive what the universe offers me. Thank you, Reesa for helping him transition. Thank you, God. Thank you, my family. Bless you.

I cannot imagine the grief the community is experiencing. I cannot imagine the grief Daniel held. He held it because he couldn't be where he wanted to be. He is free now. After his passing, we helped spiral away the dark side to the light. The side that is so fearful, the side that makes us afraid until we get so big and fearless that it melts the heaviness. Last night on the porch we burned fears, regrets, anger, and concerns in the purifying fire. Now the heart can beat freely, our freedom is close at hand. We are safe.

Your amazing willingness and ability to understand the possibility of who he was gives us great peace. We let him go in love and light and take up the challenge and responsibility to heal, not only ourselves, but our friends, family and whatever the universe calls for. Our lives are blessed to have had you here, and we will cherish every moment of our lives as we learn and continue to fulfill our purpose on Earth.

I know this will be hard to hear, to understand right now as I speak. But I want to share a truth, from the bottom of my heart, that I have conquered and transcended my greatest fear. Whatever you feel you need, from me, from Fred, from Deborah, from Dan, or from God, please ask and open your heart to receive. You deserve it. Those of you who knew Dan saw the light and fire in his eyes, the light of love, the fire and determination to share his truth.

Expressions of love in all forms from all levels have been flooding in. You will get a taste of some of these today when Dan's family and friends share their hearts. But more importantly, it is your heart that you will be attending to. In your healing is your gift.

My expectation was very high for healing. It appeared from what Kaitlin told us in her call, that the way Dan left shattered a lot of people's beliefs about the nature of reality, of life, and of what is supposed to be. Fortunately, those who spoke at the Memorial

Service the next day were able to hold the huge energy necessary for such a large group, and share with us some personal experience and insight into Dan's nature. The frequency of healing had begun.

Chapter 22

Memorial Day

In our town, we don't talk about funerals. Rather, we offer celebrations of life. In this case, it felt more like a celebration of death — an unusual terminology for a suicide.

How does one encapsulate a life in a memorial service? Whether it is the twenty-five years of one's son, eighty-five years of one's parent, or sixty years of one's spouse, it all seems to get interred in the mind and heart. What is remembered gets diluted over time. But what remains are the lessons of relationship, love, and connection.

When I attend these services, I always get to know the person being honored in a way I would never have known them before, almost as if I was being introduced to someone for the first time. Ironically, that was true even for my son, whom I had raised, hugged, fought with, and loved for these many years.

It is the heart that wants to remember. This last day of May 2010 was not only Dan's Memorial Service but the Remembrance Day for all those who have gone before us. Dan always created a big energetic picture, and that was the way IT was.

I felt Dan was somehow organizing and leading this event, but

I didn't realize to what extent until a friend described his presence. Dan was seen, in angelic form, with giant wingspread around the massive tent, overseeing a council of celestial beings. He obviously was a silent witness, but I am sure he was somehow "in charge," as those who spoke spilled out their hearts, their love, and their grief in their personal stories. The variety of expressions, tenor of delivery, and philosophical outpourings gave the sense of Dan's complexity, who he was on the planet, and perhaps who he might be as an inter-dimensional avatar.

Memorial Day of 2010 was a picture-perfect scene. Our greened-up, flowers in bloom in the back yard presented themselves as if they were prepared for a wedding. A warm, pleasant, seventy-eight degrees somehow felt comforting to the three hundred or so seated under the protective canopy with one hundred more on our deck and sprawled on blankets scattered around. A microphone projected an intimacy only a Memorial Service would allow.

The air was filled with an almost tangible, graceful presence. Dan had left the earthly realm only four days earlier with a single gunshot to the head. Although he had talked about such an event ten years earlier, I could never have accepted such a loss then.

The following presentations are remembrances that capture a feeling of Dan through the eyes of others. It is a story continuing to unfold for those of us still here on the planet.

Hosting the Memorial

Fred, the host of this life-changing event, Dan's Dad, employer, and friend, displayed an ease with surrender, gratitude, and graciousness. His welcome uplifted the community to honor and heal hearts.

Today, it is our hope that in honoring the memory of Dan, that there is an extraordinary healing that takes place for all of us. Day by day we gain new understandings that he had projects going on that we were completely unaware of. Today we will take the opportunity and begin to understand the depth of his experiences through the eyes of his family and close friends.

While listening to the recording of this tribute to a powerful soul who was instrumental in so many lives, I realized I only knew a fraction of what was and had been going on. I only recognized Dan as a physical presence with a Divine soul rather than a Divine soul with a physical presence. I learned many inspiring personality attributes that he, as a spiritual mentor and friend offered to so many. Although I wish I had known him more authentically and fully while he was on the planet, having any regret now would not serve me, him, or the learning that I need now.

Reading a passage from Maharishi Mahesh Yogi, Fred attempted to explain an important perspective about death.

When someone dies, it is not possible to understand why it had to come when it did, and there is no point in assuming responsibility or guilt. The course of action is unfathomable. However, especially for one on the path of speedy evolution, transition is purely evolutionary. Grief is natural. Allow the soul to feel loved, and that they are free to move on to their destiny. It is important to feel love and support for the departed soul, as our energy affects their evolution.

This message carries a similar meaning to the one that Dan communicated to us in his 'letter of apology,' where he asked us to honor the way he left. That message, as well as the one Hilary gave in her readiness to understand the distance that Dan created by leaving her partnership, gave me a courage that I may not have garnered alone. As Fred compassionately states, "for Dan, it was just a matter of time. We talked about this for years. He wanted to reunite with Mother Divine right away."

The importance of death being an evolutionary event, even for a suicide, seems to be very important in our spiritual community. To give up the physical presence even in love, can be a tall order. The belief that taking one's life disrupts the karmic cycle of the soul leads to the interpretation that a life meant to be fully lived is cut off. However, according to the Eastern Astrological Jyotish reading and Kaitlin's explanation, Dan's purpose was different and had nothing to do with earthly karma.

A similar message was sent by a friend who arranged a yagya (purification ceremony) for Dan to absolve him of any continuing karma or wrong doing. The report was that the special ceremony was not for Dan at all. He was fine. The spiritual blessing was meant for the rest of us, his family and community. Again, I imagine, Dan considered the ceremony necessary for those of us left here. He wasn't on the Earth to clear out past Karma. He had never been here before.

Blessings from Dan's Sister

There is something "humanly" divine and precious that came to our family in feminine form. A second child, Deborah held and continues to hold a very different energy than her brother. In her twenty-two years, during her brother's life here and in the few days that followed his disappearance, she became more aware of their differences in the name of love.

Deborah began her beautiful memorial exposition with silence and suspended breath. At the helm with microphone in hand, she opened up the flow with a deep, mellifluous Maori chant that slowly emerged from the very bottom of the Earth itself. She became an instrument of a holy, holistic vibration resonating a universal heartbeat. This ceremonial expression she learned from her spiritual mentor while she lived in New Zealand. Although no one present understood the meaning of this indigenous language, the guttural solidarity of the piece displayed an important ceremonial significance that brought forth a spirit of wholeness.

Deborah shared…

Dan and I always noticed how different we were.

I loved the Earth, and enjoyed the ancient ties with the Indigenous. As we got older, we shared more insight. I explained how I thought the laws worked here and he would bring me into an incredibly cosmic state. There was a feeling that we were opposites yet working together. He would see things from the top down and I from the bottom up. Even though he wasn't meant to continue learning about the laws here on this plane, no matter how much I wanted him to stay, I recognize that I can still rely on his support and teachings to move forward.

One day, when I wanted better insight into our dynamic, I

opened a book of Rumi and discovered what I needed to hear. It's called 'Birdwings.'

"Your grief for what you've lost lifts a mirror
  up to where you're bravely working.
Expecting the worst, you look, and instead,
  here's the joyful face you've been waiting to see.
Your hand opens and closes and opens and closes.
If it were always a fist or always stretched open,
  you would be paralyzed.
Your deepest presence is in every small contracting and
  expanding, the two as beautifully balanced and
  coordinated as birdwings."

At this point, Deborah relayed a story of when they were kids together, playing a super hero game outdoors. She was probably two and he five. She spoke to us as though she were speaking directly to him, which, in fact, she probably was, and I'm sure he was listening.

"I remember when we were really young and you pulled me into your game."

Since I didn't really know what was going on, I relied on him telling me what to do.

"Hold the sword this way, and run after the bad guy."

If I wanted to sit down because I didn't want to play anymore, he'd at first be confused, and then say *"You didn't tell me."*

Then with his creative flexibility and love toward me he'd make an instant game change.

"OK, you can be keeper of the tree."

He would incorporate everything into his world, even though it didn't fit in with the Earthly laws. Dan was only interested in the things that people really cared about and in connecting that way. As long as I stay connected with him there is huge joy. That was an energetic breakthrough that showed me a new reality of life.

Then Deborah changed direction and looked at everyone. With deep empathy for all of us she continued:

We are all so connected, so I don't see this as personal just to me. All of you here are my family. Everyone has different roles and I feel that sense of loss is what we are working on in ourselves. Since he has passed there has been a lot of shock, but looking back it all makes sense. Lots to swallow. I feel him so present with me.

He never accepted the laws here as big enough. I feel we will still be working together. I can use his support and teaching and stand here and be strong and move forward. He carried so much positive energy. He only wanted to talk about the big things, and connect deeply. As long as I can stay connected to him, I can experience joy.

It took many years for this wonderful being to truly heal from losing her only sibling. After all, she took up the courage to go to his house when I abdicated from fear. And, she left town right away to avoid having to face others treating her in a new, painfully awkward way. So, her healing was put on slow motion. Yet, now, I believe she has come full circle and has reconstructed a new, healed heart within her own body.

As written by Germaine de Stael, the eighteenth century French Romantic writer, *"Love is the emblem of eternity: it confounds all notion of time: effaces all memory of a beginning, all fear of an end."*

What does Buddha have to do with all this?

A professor and family friend opened his heart to the community with stories from his trip with Dan on a University trip to China. In addition to sharing his glimpse of Dan's inner spiritual world, he shared an important caution. While honoring who Dan was, he made sure to let everyone know that it is of utmost importance for the rest of us to fulfill our role ON the planet. It has been clear that Dan's purpose was to encourage others to be comfortable here and not avoid their purpose. This advice came from Dan even in the midst of him feeling differently about his own life.

Greetings. It's remarkable how you are all doing. I knew Dan from birth, I thought.

But, I never really had an opportunity to peek into his inner world until he joined our college trip to China.

It was in the sweet light of the holy mountains of North Central China, where twenty-seven Temples spread throughout the valleys, that I noticed his subtle presence. It was in the main temple of the Taoist Monastery.

I was fascinated by the silent, powerful attention he gave the monks, and the comfort he seemed to feel in such a holy place. As a professor casually asking Dan to share, I simply asked, "What was your experience?" Without any hesitation, he filled me in.

'It was like a welcome home party.'

In a way, I was taken by surprise, and I clammed up. I didn't want to know anymore. What he was really thinking and feeling was not something I expected to hear, so I just waited and took in the silence.

Dan didn't show up for dinner the next night. When I asked about his absence, he noted that he was just going through so much purification that he couldn't leave his room. Again, I was taken aback, but I was beginning to feel into this young man's power. I stood still inside. It wasn't until the next day that I began to feel into his heart, an experience that affected me deeply.

I wanted to see the Temple of Quan Yin. The reverence of the students so impressed the head abbot that he opened up the Temples in the outskirts of the sanctified temples.

One of the most beautiful temples had 108 flying Buddhists in the main reception. The smaller hall was populated by sculptures of the medicine masters from the Daoist lineage. This is where Daniel decided to settle in.

Again, I wanted to know more about his internal world, so I quietly but directly asked. His reply was simple and honest.

"I was just expressing my gratitude for my sister's healing from cancer when she was a little girl."

Moved to tears, I turned away, feeling the power of the humility. It was clear that there was a personal communication with Buddha, but it was not for me to know so directly. This sentiment was very powerful for me at the time, as it is now, that this was his thought, his impulse even after years had gone by from the time of her healing.

One thing I want to close with. It's a directive really coming from Dan who took his own, what I consider, precious, life. Although we have all been granted a blessing to have known Dan in all his glory while he was with us, it's not for us to follow his path away from this planet during this important time on Earth. We are not to follow his action, nor consider for ourselves the way he left, but just honor the Being that he was and is. It's our role to continue our evolution here and fulfill our karma and purpose in our physical bodies. Our role is to be here, to evolve, and to support life as we know it on Earth.

This fellow, now in tears, vulnerable to a new experience that was opening his heart, said what is in all our hearts, and what Dan actually taught and supported while he was here. Dan spent his attention offering healing messages, helping people become more comfortable with their spiritual experiences and to honor the importance of being here no matter what they needed to learn. Sometimes life is not so kind. Sometimes we are in a position to help others having a hard time, and sometimes we are in a position to ask for assistance. Whatever the case, we work it out.

It is rare to just touch down for the sake of experiencing earthly life. From my understanding, there is a karmic wheel that we are hoping to complete as we develop the refinement and awareness necessary to step out of the cycle. And so, with all the incredible stories that Dan's friends and family members express, the specific circumstance of his death does seem to be related to an unusual soul who somehow chose to be here, not to learn and play out any past karma, but just to try out earthly life and assist. Coming to terms with who he was, was not an easy task for him, and his emotional body often had to fight through his knowingness to stay.

Hilary's Perspective Shift and more

How could I love someone so much and not be with him?

When Dan told Hilary that they would be separating ways a couple of months before he left the planet, she immediately felt shafted. The anger, remorse, and sadness shot through like a lightning bolt of fury. And then, within a few minutes, she knew it was ok. It had to be.

I deeply held so much faith in him. Without much thinking, I admitted that he was an important spiritual teacher for me, as he would say about me. "You are totally family to me," and I wanted him to continue to be my guide even if we weren't together physically. Little did I know then how true this would be.

I can't even explain how much I learned from him.

Dan was a bizarre kind of person, in a good way. Even though I was in a lot of pain, I remembered our discussions about working together in the future to provide healing and spiritual guidance to those needing assistance.

Dan helped me, and continues to this day, to discover who I truly am. The Emotional Processing Technique that he taught me is so powerful that I'm propelled to share this along with my own healing work. In short, it teaches us NOT to resist emotions, but to love through them. Although I wanted to call it the DIS (Daniel Isaac Swartz) EPT, he told me to just own it for myself. No sense in carrying on an old frequency. So, I let the DIS part go, as I had to let him go, too.

Relentlessly believing everyone could get past their suffering, he'd always make sure to share that we are all rock stars. He didn't just believe it, he knew it. You can all have exactly what you want. You desire it and then just get out of your own way. If you don't do this right away, he'd say there is still some lingering resistance. Your desire is the seed of who you truly are and what you are going to have.

She now directs her words to him.

So, now I want to thank you, Dan, for teaching me all this. Thank you for holding me high in your esteem, telling me that I am the closest to Mother Divine that you ever had.

Back to us…

But now the truth must be told and understood. He needed this experience of the Divine Mother from the Universe, not just from me. If I can have a little Dan inside of me all the time, then I can always share what he taught me. He made my desire to help others bring in to their life a more fulfilled dream.

It is fascinating and rewarding that I continue to love and honor Hilary as the closest I will ever get to having a daughter-in-law. I suppose that I did my job as an earthly mother to Dan to the best of my ability. He does admit in the farewell communication that came to us through the email share, that his leaving had nothing to do with his family upbringing. That is quite a relief given that I know I could always have done better. No remorse, no regrets, only gratitude for having been his Mom here.

The concept of having a Being within that is continually guiding us is actually quite charming. Whether it be God, Jesus, Mother Mary, Mother Divine, a specific Guru, or any sentient soul in the flesh with whom we connect, it feels good, safe, and hopefully even deserved.

From my perspective, growing up Jewish with God introduced as a loving Father figure, I have always felt a protective, guiding presence surrounding me. The consequence of this is that I always had to mind my p's and q's, or else. I'm not quite sure what the "or else" was about, but I didn't really want to find out either. As you can imagine, I was mostly well-behaved, and when I wasn't, I felt a great deal of remorse.

The idea that God, a creator on the outside, can be experienced on the inside, and that we can open to such a big energy always fascinated me. It has become my belief system now, and I still feel that by regularly practicing my meditation technique and continuing to align the physical with the spiritual, the reality becomes even more palpable. That is perhaps why we are on the planet, to integrate the spiritual into the physical. But, of course, this was not the mission that Dan saw for himself. I am assuming he took the attitude as do others that we are spiritual beings having a physical experience. In any case, it does seem to work both ways.

What is our purpose here?

My challenge is to be able to expand and integrate higher frequencies of energy into my body. His challenge seemed to be the opposite, to be able to hold the dense energy in his body necessary to stay on the planet. Delores Cannon's book, "The Three Waves of Volunteers and the New Earth," gives us some additional understanding of people like Dan. Delores Cannon writes…

"In 1945, when the atomic bombs were dropped in WWII, our 'protectors' and 'watchers' in outer space saw that Earth was on a collision course with disaster. The prime directive of non-interference prevented them from taking any action, but then they came up

with a brilliant plan to save Earth and assist in her ascension. They couldn't interfere from the 'outside,' but maybe they could influence from the 'inside.' SO the call went out for volunteers to come and help. 'Earth is in trouble – who wants to volunteer?'

The native souls living on Earth were too caught up on the wheel of karma. The only hope was to ask for pure souls to come who had never been trapped on the karmic cycle."

You can decide for yourself if you are one of these volunteers. So many of us are here to help heal the Earth and support the future generations. Our thinking needs to be long term, and that means attending to our own evolution in order to support a new, earthbound, higher frequency reality. And, it is clear, there is assistance from "the other side." We are not alone.

Friends share their hearts

Avi, the very last person Dan spent the day with, had a hard time getting out his words. But he really was able to express what it was like to be with his friend. He did mention through his heaves of sadness, that Dan told him of his imminent plan.

It's been hard for me. I miss him so much.

Last week he came out to be with me on the land, to assist me with my work. Within in a few minutes he told me that he was going to leave. A shiver of fear coarsed through my body, and all that ventured out of my mouth, was "please don't."

We went to the woods as we used to do back here on this land. To help me with my work, he gave it a try to dig a hole with an awkward gas powered machine. With its cumbersome power, Dan held onto the machine and started spinning in a circle, following its lead.

"Dan, I said, stay steady. You have to resist with me as I resist the machine."

Touching shoulders we dug holes faster and faster with a speed I'd never known before. The next day when we connected by phone, he said he wanted to come back, but he couldn't.

At this point, my heart felt so tender for Avi. I had watched him grow from a busy pre-schooler into a knowledgeable arborist, chef, and steady friend. What a burdensome energy to hold on behalf of his friend! The love seemed bigger than my heart could handle, choking me up and then allowing the burgeoning tears to fall from my eyes. The blurred vision made it easier to listen further.

I've known him for a long time. He surrounded himself with very grounded people. I was his guide on the Earth. He never really wanted to go outdoors, but I'd drag him into the woods. I would never listen to his goings on about his spiritual musings. They didn't seem important to me. What was important, I'd say, is that you taste the food I make for you. To take care of yourself while you are on Earth. He was always happy I knew these things, but he didn't care.

I miss him a lot and am just really grateful that he was in my life and that I continue to realize his value.

Healing from such a traumatic loss takes time, and I honor Avi for having been there for Dan. I'm thankful that he was able to help Dan ground his energy to stay on the planet as long as he could, and for confronting the loss with honesty and courage. Some months later, Avi honored Dan by planting a small tree grove of edible fruit and nut trees in our backyard.

God, please let him go

Dan's friend, Ted, shed more light on Dan's personality as he spoke to us in a composed, and even humorous manner. It was so enlivening to be able to laugh at Dan's antics amongst such serious despairing.

It was very difficult to prove Dan wrong. He always listened, but always had a more expanded view point that you just couldn't argue with.

Lots of people are flakey, but Dan was never flakey, he was undeniably reliable. Even though he would always want to talk about ethereal beings floating around, he always kept his appointments with people.

Ted shared with dynamic enthusiasm and physical dramatics giving us all a chance to let go and laugh.

A comment that Ted made regarding our roles in Dan's life was one many felt in our hearts at this time. There was a significant understanding that Dan was always willing to be there for his friends and clients; he gave a lot. Yet, there was a nagging questions inside of some people now. "Did I give enough back? Is there anything I could have done to keep him here?" Perhaps there is something in our emotional system called guilt that keeps us in this story. But, according to my understanding of Dan's need to go "home," nothing could have kept him here.

Ted continued.

In the last few months, my girlfriend and I would sit down on the couch and listen to the music Dan liked to listen to and play with his newly formed band. One band that he liked, called Owl

City, describes where I think Dan is now. The song is called, 'The Technicolor Phase.'

I am the red in the rose, the flowers
on the blankets on your bedroom floor.
And I am the gray in the ghost that hides
with your clothes behind your closet door.

I am the green in the grass that bends back
from underneath your feet.
And I am the blue in your back alley view
where the horizon and the rooftops meet.

If you cut me I suppose I would bleed the colors
of the evening stars.
You can go anywhere you wish 'cause I'll be there, wherever you are.

I am the black in the book
the letters on the pages that you memorize.
And I am the orange in the overcast
a color that you visualize.

I am the white in the walls that soak up
all the sound when you cannot sleep.
And I am the peach in the starfish on the beach

that wish the harbor wasn't quite so deep.

If you cut me I suppose I would bleed the colors
of the evening stars
You can go anywhere you wish 'cause I'll be there, wherever you are

I researched and listened to the song on YouTube, and it did bring me to a teary knowingness. The tears were echoes of Dan's longings to be more than his human nature would allow. With head bowed in prayer, Ted implored Dan and the Lord this way.

Just keep going toward God, Dan. Listen, as I'm speaking to you now. And, I implore, you, God, make exceptions for him. Let him go, because he was such a great healer and such a great soul.

A discovery of God's location

One summer day when Dan was little, I took him out into our woods with a monitor in hand to listen for my sleeping baby's awakening moments. She was in her stroller on our deck, just out of eyeshot. Attentive to his internal world, Daniel wasn't much interested in my chatter. Suddenly, I heard the fretful murmuring of his infant sister, and I was on alert. I told Daniel he could come with me to get her, or just stay where he was, and I'd be right back. Engrossed in his stick and fantasy game, he said he would wait.

So, I quickly went to the house, whisked my little girl into my arms, and rushed back to join Daniel. As I suspected, he naturally moved out of the waiting spot while engrossed in his magical world. I wasn't concerned until I heard some whimpering a few yards away. "Mom, where were you, he sniffled," hardly aware that only a little time had passed, and that he wasn't really very far from the house.

It was clear he was feeling left alone, and to comfort him I said, "Daniel, you are never alone. God is always with you, and I wasn't far behind."

"You, mean," he said looking up in a newfound reverence, "I am standing on God right now?"

This told me something, not only about his newfound understanding, but that he was probably right. God is everywhere, not in the sky, not just outside or inside, but everywhere, an important learning from a three-year old. "Going toward God," as Ted wished for Dan, then, must be an easy task.

Courageous or cowardly: How would Dan have explained it?

Rick Archer, a true spiritual seeker, a seasoned, successful interviewer of spiritually awakening people in an online forum called Buddha at the Gas Pump (BATGAP), had a story to share that is a little different than what we had been hearing.

I had the privilege of spending two to three hours a week in a spiritual discussion group with Dan for the past few years. We were twenty to thirty people in room sharing our personal experiences of higher states of consciousness. In our mutual interaction, a churning took place that raised the energy in the room to a very high level. I would come away surcharged and feel that way throughout the week. Dan was one of the major engines of that process. When he was there, the room lit up. When he wasn't, the energy wasn't the same.

The information I will mention now, is quite different than what we've been hearing today. After my praises of Dan on Friday night, the second night of "sitting Shiva," people's feedback varied from thanking me for my uplifting words, to chastising me for being too much in my head. "How can you intellectualize such a tragic event?

You're reinforcing a wrong way of thinking."

My response to the disparity between the honoring words that have been said and the countering, discouraged feedback, is, "How would Daniel have handled this?" Dan was a master at validating peoples' perspective, and flipping it around and showing that there was a bigger perspective. Now, I find myself doing the same thing.

On one hand, Dan, that was a dumbass thing to do; on the other hand, that was an amazing act of courage and faith. "Such a loss to the world," I thought. "But, this is going to teach me a lesson for the rest of my life."

No one really has the answers even though we would all like to think we do. We all have our stories, and sometimes we fight wars over them, or fly airplanes into buildings. But they're just stories, and nobody's story encapsulates the whole reality. When Dan would listen to someone's story, he was able to say, "Yeah, I see that. Now here's a bigger picture." It would break them out of their story and elevate them to a higher level. That's what I experienced, a weekly dose of story breaking. Very powerful technique for me. And, if we could totally get rid of our stories, I think we would all be fully awakened.

I appreciate Rick for his candidness. There was some resonance with the more angry response within myself, although I knew of Dan's continual emotional conflict. In some ways, the suffering he experienced while receding from his physicality was almost more painful for me to watch than the actual consequences of the turmoil. How could I possibly stay present emotionally and even be helpful to my son. The transformational "healer" in me was suffering, too.

The Avatar fesses up

Isaac, perhaps Dan's closest friend with whom he had regular, lengthy spiritual discussions, was coming as fast as United Airlines could take him. Although he didn't make the Memorial event in person, he sent a letter by email that Rick read out loud.

Because this following piece of information was new for most, including Rick himself, he prefaced the reading with, "Take this with a grain of salt as we should take everything." Although this caused a big laugh because of the unintended double entendre, I think the humor may have gotten re-absorbed as Rick read Isaac's message. Dan had previously only shared this information with family, Hilary, and Isaac. This was the first time it became public, and only in the wake of his leaving.

Isaac Spills the Beans

I wouldn't have mentioned this while Dan was alive, because he would have been embarrassed. He finally recognized that he was an Avatar sometime a few years ago after he woke up. He never told anyone, as he never wanted to appear arrogant or confuse anyone. He explained it as a realized soul, a particle of God—that this soul didn't have any more karma it needed to work out. It's not the same experience as a soul who thinks he has to come back to free itself from a karmic cycle and become enlightened, or whatever they choose to call it.

Dan remembered his lives before birth on this planet, playing around in different realms and even being the realm itself. In learning about the Earth, he had the desire to come and help uplift the world. This is the reason he seemed to speak with undue authority on the nature of Avatars. It wasn't undue. It was from his direct experience and understanding, but he didn't want to say it that way at the cost of others not understanding, or worse, "putting me on a pedestal."

It's very simple. We're all part of God. Those who get it, don't have to come back to the classroom. But they always have to dress the part if they do and go through the process of remembering. Don't you dare put him on a pedestal. He would smack you. We are all particles of the Divine. You can't get more equal than that.

How people absorbed this information is hard for me to know. Even though Isaac seemed to know and accept this as true, I'm not sure when Dan shared this with him. My guess is that it was long before he shared it with me, which was only a few weeks before he left. Interestingly enough, when Dan did reveal himself, my response to this "news" was quite neutral. I just asked him a question or two about who knew this, and the nature of an avatar, which he described as a form of "light being," and that there were different levels of avatars. Apparently he had shared this with Fred, Hilary, and of course, Isaac, and that's about it. My response to him was, "that's great, thanks for telling me." Then, we went on with our walk to lunch.

Roseanne's Vision

The reason I write this now is that it responds to Daniel's comment that we are all part of God, and, that he seemed to convey this "reality" to those he worked with. Roseanne speaks directly to all of us as if we are all part and parcel of Dan, of God, of a totality that often gets lost in our everyday thoughts. In some sense, she is putting Dan on a pedestal, but, from my standpoint, it is couched in the blessing that higher consciousness is available to everyone.

When I look at you, I see Daniel. When I look at you, I see my-self. (Sniffle) Over the past year and a half I've talked to Daniel just about every week. When I look at you, I see what I do have. What Dan showed me is that everything that I think I want, I already have.

There have been two major forces in my life. Maharishi and the gift of meditation, and Daniel. I don't feel anyone has known me for the way I am the way Daniel has. He held such a place of under-standing and compassion. I never felt so much freedom to be myself and just say whatever I wanted to say. Monday night, I was in North Carolina and I talked to Daniel over the phone. I wasn't feeling very happy with myself. He responded to my disenchantment with, "this is really big, this is great," as he often does. And, then I started to feel better and recognized that to be true. He taught me to accept, honor and be OK with my feelings.

In some ways I feel like Dan was my Guru from a past life. The conversations were amazing and I'd have to pinch myself to see if it was real. The wisdom would just flow. Then I would leave and I couldn't remember what happened. Every week, some transfor-mation would happen and yet I wouldn't need to remember it. He was somehow sitting inside me. He's been my friend, brother, father, teacher, and my guide. And, I was supposed to talk to him today, and I have this feeling that I'm going to keep talking to him. What he gave me, and what he gave all of us is beyond space and time. I thank you for bringing him in.

It was nice to hear this, and I wondered who the thank you was for. Although I had birthed him, and Fred clearly had something to do with his existence here too, I didn't have a specific feeling that I was bringing in an Avatar, or a son that couldn't stay in his body for that matter. I still went through all the "trappings" of motherhood. The learning and gratitude, however, is not to be underestimated. So much was learned in raising him, and I'm sure that is true for all parents. Just this time around, I am having to learn about truly letting go. The gratitude is for the learning, and for having had him as a physical presence in my life for twenty-five years. Do I still "have" a son? You bet.

Jared and the Minority Justice League

One of Dan's close friends, quite shaken up, reads his words to us.

He was such an evolved and spiritual being that just the idea of him causing himself harm is hard for me to believe. When Dan was dark and down, it was hard for me. I felt like he was the only one who could listen to my concern about my existence here on the planet.

We loved movies and Dan was a man of decisions, so we watched many together that we both related to. But more importantly than our similar taste in movies, we were able to "get" each other. With our friend who came to town for this auspicious day, sitting amongst us now, we formed the Minority Justice League - she the black girl, me the gay guy, and Dan, the Jewish kid. Together we fought absolutely nothing. (laughter)

After getting to know Dan, I decided to dig deeper into Dan land.

As has been mentioned already, he had an uncanny ability to plug into the world of anyone and find a soothing solution. Conversations often turned into revelations that completely changed how we would see the world. It's impossible to say in words how much I've grown from them.

I knew Jared through both Hilary and Dan, and he epitomized the out-of-the-box creative side. When dressed as a woman at a party, and now at Burlesque shows, he was actually the most beautiful of the women. It was impossible to pick him out of the crowd unless you were aware of his costuming genius.

When I met with Jared recently, he confided with me that Dan was the first man that he ever felt comfortable enough with in order to share his deepest feelings and angsts. Dan not only provided a soothing ear for Jared, but apparently Dan confided his own dilemma with Jared who wanted to maintain a friendship. From my standpoint, that put them between a "rock and a hard place." There was little room to squeeze out of the discomfort. Jared mentioned that Dan said he didn't want to die, but that he couldn't stay in the body any longer. What a secret to burden his friend with.

The experiences of people who engaged with Dan, even though their stories take on their own personal twist, seem to have a common theme. Because they felt safe to connect deeply with one another, they became friends. Doing stuff with them would concretize their relationship.

In a dream I had after Dan left his body, I was watching a movie with him in the etheric realm. Jared was watching it with us, too. The theme was clearly superhero feats of justice, but I couldn't hear the film. I only could watch it. I'm not one to interpret dreams much, so I guess I'll never know what actually happened. Perhaps "life" after the physical body communicates silently, telepathically. I can wait for the experience!

Chapter 23

On Equality And Inspiration

The theme that came out from everyone who spoke at the memorial was that Dan was here to serve, and perhaps that was his only purpose… to serve the planet as he made the choice to touch down, to serve those living here who are willing to elevate their consciousness and add to the rising frequencies so needed at this time. His serving may certainly have affected the political and social climate, but his method was through spiritual mentoring. And, it is important to recognize that we all have our own ways and purpose to express our passions and contribute to humankind and the planet.

In a poetic expression of appreciation, one of his online clients wrote:

Dan was way wise beyond his age. Not that he was a guru one would seek, but it was he who sought — sought hearts to engage — and push them faster into depth and clarity. Dan is an evolutionary wind at my back; he shepherds me still… he slogged for hours to help me step into love, and he did; it is the source that flowed through him that I can never forget, for is not the silence of his missingness yet the best of him?

It was a disappointment and mystery to many that he chose to leave so abruptly. But, from my standpoint, I knew he felt he would be more valuable to the planet and humanity from somewhere else.

Everyone certainly has a purpose here and elsewhere. What a great blessing it is, or would be, to know what that is. Many of my clients are asking to really know what their specific purpose is. What is it that creates a passionate inspiration to serve, to live, to do whatever job is necessary and important in this time and place? Uncovering what drives us forward is a great blessing. I believe wholeheartedly that if you have the question, you'll find the answer.

I appreciated Isaac's message speaking on behalf of Dan.

We're all part of God. Those who get it, don't have to come back to the classroom. But they always have to dress the part if they do and go through the process of remembering.

Interpreted in an adamant tone of voice for Isaac, Rick read:

Don't you dare put him on a pedestal. He would smack you. We are all particles of the Divine. You can't get more equal than that.

The "equality" theme in Dan's life became clear to me when he was a young teen. The comment below is a memory I have from a visit to my folks one summer. When Daniel had grown taller than his grandmother, she, in her usual way made the comment, *"I guess I have to look up to you now."* His response was, *"I may be taller than you grandma, but I'll never look down on you."*

Chapter 24

The Aftermath: My Bedroom Retreat And The Primal Scream

My inner thoughts kept me company in my bedroom for many mornings after all the visiting of friends while sitting Shiva, the cremation, and the memorial service. I let my focused activity move into a simple, silent state. My silence was lovingly protected by friends who came over to answer the phone and the front door. People came with bouquets in hand, including the local flower shop who had come to know our address very well. People streamed toward our house as if it were a spiritual mecca to sooth their own souls, experiencing the beautiful energy that surrounds a delicate silence.

Death can provide an atmosphere of Divine silence. I slipped into that comforting space. Yet that stillness was frequently interrupted with my mental shoutings. "F… you," came way too often. No one heard it except me, and perhaps Dan. I so much wanted to be a compassionate, loving Mom and just be present for this soul who must have been tormented in the deep knowingness that he HAD to leave.

Primal Screams

My new homeopathic remedies promoted a sleepy, almost drugged response, giving me the healing opportunity to rest, sleep, meditate, and feel. Somehow, Fred was able to take care of Dan's rented house, clean it up, take out his belongings, and get the furniture ready to donate to a nearby rescue center. The expensive music studio equipment found a new home in our music room.

One afternoon, in the early days of my convalescing, I went into the music room and lovingly ran my hand across Dan's electronic drum heads. I felt an enduring love of sweetness.

When I returned to my bedroom, now alone in the house, I suddenly, without any physical or emotional warning, began to let out uncontrollable, screaming heaves of grief. On, and on, and on. After two hours, I felt drained and quieted enough to call one of my friends for her intuitive guidance. When she asked what had precipitated this behavior, I remembered running my hand over his instrument. She explained that the intense energy with which Dan lived and expressed in his music was embodied in his electronics, and that Fred could ground that energy for me. Just this knowledge gave me instant relief. I stopped the noisy crying, calmed down, and fell into a deep sleep. That evening Fred took care of my request.

Of course, I had to test it out the next day. I ran my hand over the drum heads as I had done the previous day, and found that that energy had been neutralized. My grief never again came out in unrelenting heaves, more like tears of gentle sadness. And, that was minimal. I just allowed myself to feel and heal.

Chapter 25

Holding The Space For Others' Healing

What does that mean, holding the space for others' healing? In this instance, I had the need to explain who Dan was, the circumstances that led him to take his life, and give it the full spiritual significance I felt he deserved. I am not sure Dan would have felt this necessary, but, after all, I was his Mom.

For a year and a half, I spoke to my friends and friends of Dan, privately over lunch, during walks, and during spontaneous meet ups at the grocery store or elsewhere. Those who were open experienced some great relief at the truth according to my sharing. Probably the most important part of this exchange was that they saw that I, his Mom, was okay. Their emotional concerns were soothed, and the fear of discussing the event was ameliorated. We felt so connected with one another.

Although it took me a while to go out in public, to integrate the loss of my special son, to mentally transition from having two kids to one, to being the mother of a suicide, and having to put up a front of not minding the projections from others, I took that step after a summer of healing. And these conversations that I had must have helped me along with others to close the wounds of distress.

Not Quite Ready: Nature's Gifts

As nature would have it, when I felt I could muster the courage to go forth into public, a bee decided I was invading its space and poked its stinger multiple times into my forehead. My face blew up to such a degree, that when I looked into the mirror, I honestly didn't recognize myself. It looked like I had been wailing uncontrollably, non-stop for many weeks. I was unwilling to risk such an image for public consumption.

When I took a picture of myself with my phone and sent it to my daughter who had escaped to Hawaii, she could only find the humor in the ridiculous image. In some way, that gave me pleasure as she still had quite a journey of her own healing ahead.

Once out and about with usual walks, I would often come upon a lone feather. A bird's gift would literally fall from the sky at my feet when I thought of Dan. It usually appeared when my heart was down, feeling a "missing" kind of sadness. Sometimes, I would immediately discover the feather on the ground; sometimes it would just drop out of nowhere. Never did I see the bird from which it fell.

Out on a "first" date

My first evening out came sometime during the fall of 2010, a few months after Dan's departure. My husband and I were sitting in our favorite seats for a local stage production of the Sound of

Music. After a number or two, I couldn't endure the sweet tones of music filling the hall. The last time I saw Dan in public with his friends Ted and Mary to the right front of where I was currently sitting, they were enjoying a dance gala that his girlfriend had organized. It gave me pleasure to see him supporting her. My eyes kept gazing in that direction until my stomach couldn't handle the memory. I walked out in tears, and left my strong, balanced husband alone to finish out the evening.

Teaching again

So, I gave myself more time to heal, and in a few more weeks, I felt ready to start teaching. This focus was a good way for me to begin with what feels like my purpose on the planet, to help others transform their energy and teach them to facilitate a powerful, self-healing process.

During an Empowerment Process workshop, one of my friends and a student in the group was willing to be the recipient of a learning demonstration. When I asked this fellow, someone of my generation, what was foremost on his mind, he hesitated a bit. With gentle coaxing, I learned that he had never really made closure with Dan's death. Apparently, they had been friends, something I hadn't known, and I assured him that this "issue" up for transformation was just fine, even with me being the facilitator. I was totally okay with it.

By the end of the weekend, he confessed to me that it was worth taking the workshop just for the relief he felt generated by that particular transformation. He took the opportunity, courageously I might add, for closure and healing.

Chapter 26

A Cosmic Invitation For Closure

Something caught my eye. I don't usually read the classifieds in our local town's newspaper. Mostly because I'm not looking to buy or sell anything, so why bother seeing what others advertise just for the fun of it. I'm too practical.

However, this particular time my eyes landed on an ad for a music student. "No kidding," I thought, as I'd been entertaining singing again. It had been a few years since my weekly lessons and a dozen public performances, and this ad was emphasizing musical theater. Seemed like fun.

So I called the phone number and left a message. When the instructor's wife called back, she set up an appointment with Joe. "Where should I come?" was my next question. When she told me the address, a sinking feeling flooded my entire body...this was the house Dan rented when he took his life a couple of years before.

Although I made the appointment, I wondered if I had the courage to keep it. Lots of emotions coursed through me, but I kept going forward until the time came. And, I went.

So far so good as I approached the porch steps. I walked up, knocked on the door, took a deep breath, and, with no hesitation, only anticipation, entered.

The door opened. I stepped in. Immediately, a huge, loving light "presence" surrounded me. The air was so pure and magnificently sweet, and all I could feel was expansive love and happiness. What an unexpected blessing.

The rest of the meeting seemed a bit inconsequential as I floated around in bliss at the knowledge of Dan having lived here. As it turned out, I took the initiative to interview Joe rather than him asking much about my musical background. Although I could see that he had lots of music around, I learned that he couldn't play the piano well enough for me to vocalize much, and he kept talking about doing big musical performances that did not really make sense to me. But I gave him a check for five lessons, and kept the judgmental observations to myself.

One, two, and three weeks went by, and I never heard a word from him. When I finally called, I learned that he had left town to support his ailing father, and that was the end of my supposed new career!

I felt fine about all this, especially when after asking for it, I got my check back in the mail. I can only say that it must have been that a divine being wanted me to be comfortable experiencing Dan's former abode. Was it Dan, himself? How could he place an ad in the paper when he could not pay for it where he was now? The thought amused me.

Now when I pass by this little house, I feel waves of bliss rather than feeling trepidation.

Chapter 27

Jyotish Revelations: Dan's Life Predictions

It is interesting that the Eastern Astrology reading I found dated February 2000, turned out to be quite accurate, yet never put a cap on Dan's life. Of course, that is fully appreciated and appropriate in my eyes. I do not think it is anyone's right, in all integrity, to suggest that anyway.

I filtered through my notes, as I was the scribe during this meeting, and I will share what makes sense to me. I don't have knowledge of Jyotish myself, so this commentary will only be through my interpretive language as a lay person. I do know that a reading involves nine planets, twelve houses of their placement and twelve signs that describe the natural tendencies of the stars. That's it.

I'll start from the top. Dan is said to have had charming speech and musical ability. Well, that's clear! He liked to talk as long as it met his criteria of "deep" spiritual conversation. His Jyotish reader mentioned that he will be comforting, uplifting and powerfully healing for others. I guess that is what the spiritual mentoring turned out to be.

He did teach himself to play the guitar, belting out words with a haunting meaningfulness in his usual intense fashion. According to the read, his voice had the effect of creating order to the environment.

Another quality indicated that he maintained a good business sense. During his time here, he made sure that he handled money wisely, and was more of a saver than a spender unless it was for his creative well-being. He did buy nice recording equipment and a laptop gamer that apparently many had never seen the likes of. One young techy said of this computer which we still have in our house, "I've never seen so much power in one machine." I can only imagine what he must have paid for it.

When I finally decided I could part with it and sell it, of course it was outdated. Now Fred and I connect it to my desktop and use it to play movies on the big TV screen, which, by the way, we also inherited from Dan. It seems weird to say that we inherited something from a son, but I guess that is the reality. One day when I thought I could tell what he was thinking, I casually mentioned that it was not natural for an offspring to leave before his parents. No response came forth, of course.

If he had lived on, the chart in his second House of Wealth indicated that he would always be protected, comfortable and probably wealthy. When he did leave, he was in his own house, paid all his bills, and left a savings that we offer as a Daniel Swartz Memorial Fund. I have the pleasure of deciding where to apply the donation each year. Now, several years later, he is still contributing money to a cause that is here on the planet. I guess that is what inheritances are meant for. As far as being protected and comfortable, that goes without saying.

Next, my notes indicate his life was often in the grip of Rahu (one of the nine planets, one of the two that is unseen and often causes confusion). Extremes, dramatic feelings and inhibition were to pervade. He would live with flare. Yet, because Rahu is exalted and in a happy place in his chart, he would know that any "big deal" amounts to nothing. This is what he said in a written, online mentoring conversation we discovered.

In terms of the no-big-dealness, it's like going through life without having any arms. And then, one day, you realize you HAVE arms. And, you can start to use them. It's the most amazing end all be all, a whole new world experience. But, after some time, we start to accept that that's just the way life is, and we go on to live our life – with arms. So, I can really appreciate having arms, but with the no big dealness, comes the ability to learn how to play guitar.

That's their usefulness. This is, in many ways, a perfect analogy about any spiritual experience. The acceptance of them fully brings about the acceptance that they are simply a part of life, and they can really serve us the way they were meant to. It's nice when it's flashy and all, but integrating it is even better.

It seems Dan had four planets in his house of speech, which apparently is very powerful. Another side to speech is listening with the heart. The interpretation was that he could be empathetic from a distance, intelligent with teacher-like abilities, and speak with good intuition and instincts, which all added to the bliss of his life.

Here is a little Jyotish language for those who understand it. In the words of Dan's chart reader, *"Jupiter, aspecting planets from the eighth house makes you a good person. This position tells us that it adds wisdom to your desires, knowledge to your wishes, and hidden esoteric knowledge to daily existence. This all adds something evolutionary to your flamboyancy."*

At this point, our Jyotishi mentioned that Mother has the tendency for esoteric knowledge. (What a surprise!)

Here is where it gets more interesting.

Dan is told, according to my notes, that he has a need to get beyond the planets so as to not be attached to anything–that he finds himself separate from his feelings. He has the ability to witness the impulse where there is a cushion between the Self and the non-Self. He is able to distinguish between who "I" am and influences from the outside on the personality.

In a writing derived from one of his online mentorings, Dan addresses this topic in a section called "Enlightenment is not a Function of the Personality."

We are all here in this Creation like children playing in a giant sandbox. What if the child makes a mistake? Does it matter? What does that even mean in the context of playing in a sandbox? There's nowhere to go and nothing to do in terms of obligations. There is everywhere to go and every-

thing to do in terms of exploration and fun. So what does a mistake even mean in that context? Do I make mistakes? As much as a child playing in a sandbox does I suppose.

I think there is a constant gift of grace being given. It's only about how much openness we allow ourselves to have in order to receive it. No matter how big our container gets, it will continue to overflow.

My take on this is the advent of a very big LOVE coming through, a love that is always forgiving where everyone is treated gently as a child in a sandbox. There is never any judgment or concern about actions being in accord with the higher, more developed Self. I appreciate writing these words as I know the message is pertinent for my own personality and spiritual development.

The final words from the Jyotishi in my notes are chilling to me. The future outlook certainly played out in Dan's plans.

Be creative, be an organizer, don't be afraid to fail. Transcend the gripping qualities of your own energy.

And, that he did.

Chapter 28

Finding Peace

It is hard for me to actually remember the exact feelings the days after Dan's disappearance from my life. When I go back and read my "letters" to him, I realize how full my heart actually was.

I must have traversed the full range of emotions. They included freak outs and anger, to feeling blessed at having had a son who was also a "light being" in my life. I guess that would translate into a soft demeanor of happiness and bliss, if you can imagine that possibility.

Here's what I wrote on May 29, two days after Deb and his Dad found him.

This morning I am so full I can barely contain myself. The Bliss is so profound, the light so bright that I hope to be expanded enough to carry the shine!

Dan kept every promise to me. He was looking forward to sharing more and more of himself and his knowledge that was so precious to him. I get it! Kaitlin completely put it into perspective, so much so, that everything Dan ever said makes total sense. I not only accept, but deeply know. I am in peace for maybe the first time in my life. Thank you for this incredible gift.

What was the promise? I guess it was that he always kept his word, that I would be privileged to understand that I live in a very expanded inter-dimensional world that includes him, and that he came and left to satisfy his need to be an earthling for a while.

The phrase, "everything Dan ever said makes total sense," means that everything was put in perspective for me, all at once. That is quite a gift in itself. What he said included not just his take on spiritual knowledge that expanded my thinking about who I am, but casual remarks that kept me in the loop of his temporary visit here.

His response to, "You'll never need us to buy you a new car," (since he would now be able to afford it for himself), came forth as, "I'll never need a new car," and, "I'll never be marrying Hilary," were circumstantial memories that nagged at me until the time they really did make sense. These remarks should have made it clear this was his last earthly vehicle and romantic partnership although I refused to accept the consequences of his intention. He kept his promise to himself at least.

And, what's this about being fully at peace? The way I would like to explain it is that holding in my feelings with an almost bursting energy throughout his life, especially the few weeks before he left, was excruciating for me, to say the least. During this time of fear while Dan was trying to stay grounded and in his body, he was like a human sponge absorbing the fear and pain from the planet. When he said to me, "Mom, you can't imagine the fear that I am experiencing," in my usual way of trying to make it ok, I said I thought I could. Not true.

He was clearly receding. I could see it in his face, softening, becoming more translucent. I could feel his need to be grounded in order to keep a physical body.

Continuing the posthumous letter directed to him..

I look forward to your teaching. I feel the healing of the community…the work is just beginning. I'll carry on. More healing today, tonight, tomorrow, Monday, and the ripples go on forever. I love you. Thank you for all your blessings.

It is interesting that I felt his leaving gave me a confidence that my learning would continue on, and that my grieving didn't seem to be an interminable emotional burden. I have to admit, years later, the need for grieving has pretty much left me, probably even many years ago. And, my learning does continue with my evolutionary growth.

Many people say to me that one never gets over losing a child. Yes, my reality has permanently changed, but emotionally I actually feel more at peace. His transition and transformation feels more like a blessing rather than a loss. But for those who hold the fear of a loss and project how I might be feeling inside, I appreciate the concern. If my being okay helps them, I am a willing participant in their healing.

Chapter 29

Visions From The Other Side

How we all receive messages from the spirit world is different for each of us. I have never received a downloaded message from a dimension beyond. Dan's messages come from others who seem to have a unique ability to perceive. Those messages have served as energetic boosts and healings for me. In the earlier days closer to the event, I longed to hear about Dan making his presence known to others to verify his continuing existence.

A message which I expressed on his Memorial Day was that although I had Dan's blessing to go through my own grieving process, I also wanted to feel valuable as a healing support to family, friends, and friends of Dan. Some took advantage of that desire and would engage in discussion about my feelings, their feelings and our knowledge. Other people just kept their anger, remorse, sadness, and whatever else they felt, inside, to deal with it as they could.

I am not one to generally "see" visions from the more subtle arenas. People often ask me if I "see" Dan. In all honesty, I have to say, "Not really." When I ask others if they talk to their friends or family members on the other side, sometimes they tell me they do. I am happy for them, and I don't look for that experience. My experience is that I feel his presence now and then. It is usually a surprise in the sense that I am not looking for him. Sometimes, I feel it is his desire to just check up on me. I always honor how I can hug a light being. For me, it is a perpetual hug that never gets lost in time and space.

My unexpected vision

Over thirty years ago, a friend's baby died within a few weeks after the birth. At the time, I was newly engaged to be married. In anticipation of having my own children, I loved watching my friend fill out as she grew in expectant mother stature. Soon, I would see her carrying a front snuggly, proudly sporting her protected baby. Then, one day, no snuggly, no infant in arms. Although I did not know the details at the time, I felt very sad about this loss. She and her husband left town, and the story resumes years later, five years after Dan left.

Apparently, the couple had moved back to town, and when I ran into her, she inquired how my children were doing. Without hesitation I told her about Dan. She offered compassion, as is the common response, and I assured her I was fine. Then, I questioned her, for the first time, about her loss years earlier.

She was explaining to me some details of the event when the conversation was interrupted by an apparition of a beautiful young woman. She just appeared before my eyes. As I thought this to be an otherworldly visit, and I immediately asked my friend if I could describe my vision. Her acquiescing smile let me know that this request was a "yes." I described flashing bright eyes of a young woman with long, silky dark hair draped over an elegant, white seraphim-like gown. I felt so grateful to be in the presence of this otherworldly Being who was so loving and seemed so real.

"Could this possibly be your daughter?" I asked. "Oh yes," she smiled and acknowledged that this is exactly the way her sister described her. I felt relieved that I was not the only one to whom this beauty would appear, and that her Mom recognized this description. Otherwise, I would have been reluctant to have honored the experience.

In the next instant, I received more information, which I immediately received permission to share. "It appears that Daniel and she are friends in their world and even have some work to do together." I was wondering if disembodied beings actually got married in another world, but I kept this query to myself. What I found interesting was that, in addition to having this lovely visitation, I became privy to Dan's relationship with this beautiful divine soul. Although I am not sure exactly the source of this information, it was received innocently and fully, and we both felt a wave of sweetness and joy as if our kids were still on the planet, or at least, were still part of our lives.

Other's Visions of Dan

The experiences that do fascinate me and seem helpful to my connection with Dan are those in which others see him in some form or other and tell me about it.

Right from the start he was recognized by a friend shopping in our supermarket as a Being requesting that a candle be lit to help in his transition. The message was to help him "right away." At the memorial service he was seen in angelic form with giant wings spread around the perimeter of the tent heading up a spiritual council. On our porch two nights before, he was witnessed dividing into infinity. Another confirmation of his reality was when a painter, working at our house that summer, mentioned that he would see Dan as a star formation at our house entrance. This acknowledgement fascinated me as I remembered Dan's comment about being a constellation. In other instances, I learned that he was available to help healers in their missions. And, according to Hilary, he continues to be one of her spiritual, personal guides on a regular basis.

The fact that I became aware of these events is a bit uncanny for me since the information arrived without my asking or expecting it in any way. However, it was necessary for my wellbeing in the early days of his leaving, and he had promised in the letter received by our friend in consciousness that he would be there for all of our healing. I think it would be a grave disappointment if I did not believe that these people's experiences were real!

Lynette's powerful healing with Dan

I was alerted to a situation that turned into a tremendous healing for Lynette, and for me once she was able to share the story. Early on after his exit, Dan showed up for one of my dear friends, who lives in New York City. Since the visitation came only a few weeks after he left, I felt grateful for the information. It was not easy for her to put her experience into words. It took several weeks and my continued prompting for her to come up with the ability to express her powerful experience.

I met Lynette as a long-distance client nearly twenty-five years before and have had the privilege of meeting with her in New York during my visits there. We stay in touch, and she continues to explore her own subtle nature that is so delicate, yet expressive in her life. She is an artist and an architect, and experiences life as a multidimensional reality. She is a healer in her own right, and I respect her abilities to continually discover new perspectives and ways of functioning. Dan's visit on July 2, 2010, was unexpected, revealing, and healing.

Dear Janet,

I hope you and your husband are having a peaceful weekend. Finally sitting down in a quiet space to finish an email to you… reflecting on my experience with Daniel's energy from earlier this month. I would have loved to put it together sooner for you…it has taken so much longer than I would have anticipated or chose…and there has been so much energy, such a powerful emotional surge, which has been overwhelming at times. The whole thing vibrated with release and relief, yet it was so powerful and so deep I could barely hold it and process it. This has been helping me to remember that with great pain and loss, there is an ineffable mystery, a divine presence behind it. Sometimes you feel it right away, sometimes it takes a while to surface. I hope this enriches your experience of loss and brings you a small measure of warmth.

It was July 2, a Friday evening. I had been in Midtown that evening and took the long walk back to Chelsea. I felt listless once back, and put on some music: "Interpol," a kind of Indie rock band.

There was a surge of grief and pain that arose in me about death and loss, which I'd been processing. It was partly due to finding out about your son's passing, and also in part to do with some intuition regarding my mother's physical frailty. Despite my not knowing Dan well and having spoken with him on the phone as his client only on one occasion, his passing affected me deeply. I went into the bedroom and listlessly sat down on the carpet with these emotions welling up.

All of a sudden, I felt there was something in the room with me. An energy, a being. I can only describe it as a kind of radiance, a kind of light energy with an electric outline. It was similar to an energy field described by a light or by a constellation.

I don't have any other words to describe this being. It was crouched down next to me. It felt glowing, gentle, and safe. I took it to be Daniel. The emotional quality was like someone laying their head in your lap in a tender, consoling way.

My mind was blown, and I was in a kind of elevated awe. There was a telepathic communication, an exchange. I don't have language or words for these things.

At some point he drew a rectangle with his finger that opened a doorway or window, a kind of vibrational gateway, which I could see through. He showed me how much light was on the other side. The light was SO bright, beautiful, clear and crystalline pure white with many, many colors shimmering and embedded within it, all pale pastel, varying vibrancies, full of hope. The brightness was love. That was conveyed in a very definite way!

The words BRIGHT and LOVE here were absolutely interchangeable.

This was so undeniable. It was the first time I could feel and experience light AS love, the light WAS love. IS love. I could feel the radiance as a state that was constant, pure, holding steady. I had not known this before except intellectually. It was also conveyed that the light was "human aura material...a communal energetic balance from within."

The whole thing was so beautiful, surreal, intangible, and amazing. At some point I internally started to question the reality of this. At that moment, a voice said, "It's a quarter to one." I went to check the time, and there it was clearly...a quarter to one. That was my validation in the physical.

The entire experience lasted maybe an hour, or slightly more. There were other things conveyed, not all of which I managed to put down. Mental imagery shown. To have courage and fortitude, like a lion. That light resolves situations, cleans things up, like finger napkins or bounty. There were also the words, "go to the other side of the door to know." Suggestions that I could open an energetic transom and pull words through higher energies. That it will "pick up the tab in your life." I am still deciphering this.

The overall theme was conveyed as THE BEST IS YET TO COME with the word BEST as an energetic overlay of the words BEST/BLESST/BLESSED. At the end there was a thought form conveyed of the word grace on top of the word grave and a kind of energetic signing off. Over and out. The final message: THE LIGHT IS HERE!!! Wonder where we are?? WE ARE IN IT!

Thank you so much for what you have shared with me in the years I have known you.

Love, Lynette

p.s. Writing this down, I realized in hindsight that the band In-terpol's two CD's I had, an Indie post punk band I never associated with spirituality at all, were titled "Turn on the Bright Lights," and "Our love to Admire."

Very coincidently, this music was the same music that, un-known to Lynette, was featured in the background of Ted's movie, Kappa, in which Dan had played the masked demi-god. I googled the group, and found that they still make albums and travel exten-sively worldwide. A web description of an Interpol piece fits Dan's personality to a T. The review goes like this.

This song is a masterpiece! It's all about how a man struggles in a relationship with another person within the constraints of the chaotic and violent nature of the world he lives in, a theme which is very well reflected metaphorically in the way the song is musically built. As the tension gets higher, the guitar player reaches the higher notes on the scale. The song 'ends' in a triumph as one of the surfers achieves his final goal. But it doesn't really end since waves depicted in the video will forever continue their way to the shore.

In listening to the group, I realized how much Dan was influ-enced by them. He wrote, played and sang a beautiful piece him-self called "Crystal Echoes," which he put on a CD that he made for me on Mother's Day that year. He also included his version of "Knocking on Heaven's Door," which at times still comes over my car radio. It stirs my heart, and a soft, ethereal memory emerges whenever I hear it.

Since Lynette mentioned in her report that she "took it (the presence) to be Daniel," I asked her to describe him physically.

How could she have known that it might be him? My heart wanted to be certain. When I asked her, she described him exactly - very tall, curly reddish-brown hair, soft brown eyes, big smile. My heart melted.

I made another observation as I read Lynette's words. They seemed so similar to the kind of conversation he had during his online discussions. Now, years later, I am learning more about how he thought and who he was as much as I can fathom. I am certain I will never fully understand who he really was, at least not while I am in this physical body.

A photographic vision: the ball of light

In 2012, Daniel would have had a ten-year high school celebration. His friends wanted him represented with photos and sayings on a poster, so I fulfilled the request. I am not sure how much of what he wrote was understood, but somehow he did have a place in this group. In any case, here is a picture of the poster with the photos and his quotes that follow in the text.

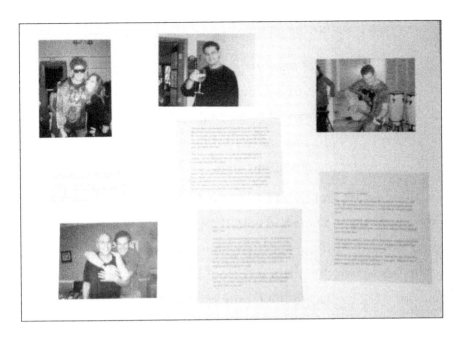

I've finally accepted my path at helping people spiritually and working with them through business consulting.

I've gotten into modes at certain points in my life where literally anything was possible. I would influence the environment and people's thoughts and actions through my energy. There have been times when I've been clairvoyant. I think that a lot of people have had experiences like that.

I think there is a constant gift of grace being given, and it's only about how much openness we can have to receive it. It will always fill us until we are full, no matter how big the container gets, and then overflow.

The point of Enlightenment is not the relative experience it creates, but the realization that the relative experience is completely beside the point.

The body is not separate from everything else. Just as we are our bodies, we are also everything else. Our bodies are not really our boundaries. It doesn't mean that life doesn't have a structure, it's just that the appearance of the structure as being limited is an appearance only.

The class apparently had a fine time connecting with each other after many years. Some had gotten married, some had established amazing careers, some were living here, and most were now out of town, with Dan, the furthest. I would have enjoyed seeing them, and we were invited to the family picnic. But my husband and I did not feel to be present. Dan had left only two years earlier, and I thought that too much attention would be in my direction. People still felt "raw" from the event, and we did not have a physical body represented at the gathering. No Dan at our side.

Some weeks later a class photo was sent to me by one of his classmates who had a question. Just to the left of a friend was a clear ball of light that carried the semblance of a face. It appeared that Dan had decided to be present. His friend asked if it was possible that it might be Dan who showed up for the photo. I was taken aback for a couple of reasons. Firstly, that this fellow would have had that idea, and secondly, that he was probably right. It was quite amusing to me and my husband. Who would have guessed that Dan would have cared.

Classmate's Dream

During the days of the class reunion, I was happy to run into a few classmates who had come to town. One gal, with whom I had a nice exchange, later messaged me on Facebook. She shared a dream reminiscent of experiences by those open to his love.

Hi Janet,

Just wanted to let you know it was so nice seeing you in the grocery store the other day and hearing how you're doing with everything.

I also wanted to let you know that I had a very sweet dream with Daniel last night. In the dream I had this near drowning experience and was back at a house afterwards. All of the sudden this tall guy appeared and walked through the door. I did a double take and then realized that it was Daniel. He was tall and radiating light with this huge smile on his face. I just said, "Oh, my gosh, it's you" and gave him a hug. It was such a sweet, deep, heart opening hug. I asked him how he was doing. He said that he was so good and so much happier where he was now. We talked a little bit about the things that you had told me. Then he just kind of disappeared. I woke up feeling happy and love in my heart.

If all dreams could end with a heart opening hug like this, the world would be a better place. She apparently knows how to "hug a light being."

Chapter 30

New Perspectives As The Journey Continues

The continuance of healing requires an ongoing openness to change. We also need to stay in the present and recognize that the present is the next moment's past, and the future is the next moment in the next moment. Life's events are continually changing. The only non-changing element is our absolute stability within.

My belief, given this knowledge and Dan's found writings, is that Dan had stabilized this non-changing field in his awareness.

I think the major challenge in moving into higher consciousness is the integration process which is what Dan was dealing with.

When we were sorting out the materials Dan left behind, I noticed that he would go through time periods of processing his concerns on an almost daily basis. Having been in the "business" of transformational work since 1994, I find it to be extremely rare that anyone can process and integrate their "issues" as quickly as he seemed to.

I discarded his many notebooks in which he recorded his

transformational processings. I felt they were personal to him and none of my business. However, one record caught my eye, so I saved it. His statement for healing his opportunity for transformation, was "I keep my heart open and feel a constant love of the infinite." This was dated October 1, 2005. His interim statements dealt with letting go of ego attachments, to accept the present time and fulfill his heart's desire.

In this unending journey, Dan continued his inner search for who he was. Dated December 1, 2009, fulfilling an assignment from the book, "the Artists Way" which he read and discussed with a community of friends, he wrote to himself,

> *Dear Artist Self,*
>
> *Thank you for unlocking the magical world of creativity and emotionalness and really following though. I'm so proud of you, and so blessed to have you in my life.*
>
> *Lots of love, Dan*

The gift of perspective, for him, was to find a way to express who he was during his first, and mostly likely last visit to this planet. For all of us, the gift is that once we can recognize life in its true, current context without the stresses, clouds, and confusions from the outside and integrate the learnings from our own inner journeys, we become a rock on the soil, the eye of the storm, the everlasting soul that doesn't become overshadowed by change. Healing can be instantaneous as we remain secure within ourselves. What a laudable goal.

Recognitions on retreat

Two months after Dan's retreat, I went on one of my own at a Retreat Center a couple of hours from home. I had gone away in the past like this to rest in my silence and open to a more Divine place within my own heart.

I thought it would be ideal to spend a few days away after Dan left, and after I had become somewhat used to having him be on a "permanent vacation." The silence was easy, as I was the only guest during that week before their weekend events. Surprisingly, the angst of loss did not seem to predominate my few days of "silent" thought. From my journal:

The 'I' of who I am does seem to be the same over the years. When I try to discover that permanent reality, there is no trying, no place to go, no distance. I like the idea of no distance in time and space because it keeps me close to Daniel, and in reality, would allow me to be one with my own son.

I wonder if this phrase is what Christians truly seek with Jesus. I am always surprised that they pray to Jesus as if he were a separate being from God. And we, as Jews, seem to pray "outwardly" to make the connection. I guess I have more to learn about this.

There is something about this retreat center that gets it though… uniting man and God, Earth with Heaven, and the soul essence with the spirit of the Divine Self. Anyway, that's my take on it.

I light the candle in reverence to the eternal Light, the flame that never goes out (even if I have to extinguish it when I leave the room.) There's something sacred about being the only Being in the twenty-room guesthouse. I am my own Guest. How charming.

Here's a toast to myself!

TO ME:

Honor, never resent

Bless, never condemn

Uplift, never denigrate

Let go, never hold on

Be aware, never die

Unite, never separate

The "whys" never matter. Cause and effect are matters of the mind. The focus is on the heart. It leads. It bridges. It is made of Divine Essence, yours and mine.

Chapter 31

Reflections On Death And Dying

It is not the concept of death or even my experience with death that challenges me. The emotional challenge is maintaining a heartfelt connection that is never lost, even in the face of the physical disappearance. But the eyes are also in our mind's eye, and we should be able to see beyond what is in front of them.

One of my favorite passages honoring the internal reality comes from Helen Keller, whom I have always loved from the day I met her through her story. I felt honored to have heard her speak during a live talk on the radio before she left the planet.

There is in the blind as in the seeing an Absolute which gives truth to what we know to be true, order to what is orderly, beauty to the beautiful, touchableness to what is tangible. If this is granted, it follows that this Absolute is not imperfect, incomplete, partial... Thus deafness and blindness do not exist in the immaterial mind, which is philosophically the real world, but are banished with the perishable material senses. Reality, of which visible things are the symbol, shines before my mind. While I walk about my chamber with unsteady steps, my spirit sweeps skyward on eagle wings and looks out with unquenchable vision upon the world of eternal beauty.

The reality of Dan's disappearance was something I was in some way prepared for. It did not lessen the shock of immediate loss and the need for a big adjustment devoid of pain and grief. However, when I felt into the situation, it was the last few weeks of his recession and fear that ate at my heart. That took a longer time to heal as it continued to plague my memory. To placate the internal disturbances, I wrote to him daily after he passed, swallowing homeopathic remedies that took the bite out of the emotional wound, and continued on a healing path.

Death itself, as reported by those who have had near-death experiences, is very freeing and generally indescribably beautiful. Although Dan needed help getting to where he thought he was going, back to Divine Mother in order to carry that big energy he wrote about in high school, he got what he needed. Those who do "see" beyond the physical reality tell me that he always carries that big, blissful smile.

In one of Dan's online mentoring sessions, a fellow suffering from confusion and pain asked, "How can you talk a snowman into loving the sun?" Dan's response, in his usual way of seeing the bigger picture, replies,

Nothing sounds more wonderful to me than melting in the sun. It's not that you die. It's that you simply realize that you never were.

Easy and blessed as my life has been, a life of immense love, good health and financial security, it is also a waiting game. Even though I am attached to my body, my husband and daughter, I intrinsically know that releasing the bond of physical reality is miraculously freeing. In addition, I believe that once freed of my earthly casing, my son will be readily available to greet me as I cross over and adjust to my new reality. So, I am expecting, rightly or not, this will be my experience when my time comes.

Meanwhile, still fortunate to maintain a healthy body, I am committed to going forward with patience and purpose, compelled to do my service here on earth.

As I embrace my own journey here and now, I seem to receive whatever I need wherever it comes from, all in the right timing. I have grown to trust this, and my intuition serves me in my life and in the life of those who come to me for intuitive and transformation work.

If life is a dream, I am the dreamer. My Creator is far bigger than my individuality and the roles I play out lifetime after lifetime. I hope to offer healing from wherever I land and be thankful for playing my part in this amazing journey.

A final thought

Although I am not one to just pray, I like the message the following invocation offers. The message seems to be for all of us, on this side and the other. The love that "lies ahead of you" is something that must lie within. This poetic statement gives us the feeling of Death being "alive," a part of the natural cycle of evolution. After all, we smile and invite birth, so why not do the same as the cycle continues? A prayer from Wistancia Stone gives this precious perspective:

Invocations to the Light

When Someone dies –
At this time of departure from the physical body, I invoke
rivers of Peace to flow
into the minds of those who would be in surprise or in
bereavement.
I ask that a bridge from the mind into the Heart be built
by Angels
who carry the deeper meaning of this experience.
I invoke the angels of Death to stand guard and resonate
the understanding of death
as a passage into another dimensional aspect of Life and
not the ending of Life.

I invoke the Soul's wisdom which holds the secret of Life
and Death.
Let the Soul's remembrance stir through you now and
flood your Beingness
with conscious application of ancient memories retained
in your heart.

Let the process known as Death be known deep within
you for what it IS
and for what it IS NOT. Let fear and remorse be no more.
Instead let be created an understanding of this:
The Spirit of the departed is beginning a new Initiation

which is cause for Celebration.
Within the unfoldment into Oneness, we all grow towards unity.
Unity holds inherent within it, the embrace of Re-Union.
To the one who has left the body, let the door to the heart chamber fly open
as your feet touch the gossamer ladder upon which you tread.

May you ascend this ladder into Greater wisdom and Understanding.
May you see the five letters PEACE that are written in golden rivulets of tranquility
as you journey toward a fuller expression of self.
Release yourself now into the Love that lies ahead of you.
Amen.

EPILOGUE

I often wonder about my current ongoing relationship with Dan.

When I'm asked by strangers "how many children do you have?" I inevitably say "two". I did birth twice.

We all live in our own subjective thought world with beliefs that form our ideas about physical and non-physical presence. As I continue to learn of Dan's activities through other's experiences with him, I wonder if I will ever have direct contact with him. Mostly, it doesn't matter, because I often feel his presence and the hug is never ending.

Maybe there is no such thing as loss, except on planet earth, where we experience the full range of emotions. The journey is mine, yours, and everyone's. You are you, I am I, and we are all connected, here and beyond.

In a writing class, five years after Dan left, I was to create a letter to someone. I chose Dan. This is what I wrote:

Dear Dan,
What the "H" am I thinking?
I am always aware of you, yet you are a swirl of a cloud in the sky.

You are a pain in my heart, a gleam in my eye.

You are a saint and a fool. All at once. Is that the condition of life?

I imagine you are everywhere. Like the time you divided in front, or rather behind our very backs, and you allowed me to carry a tail of grief that needed to be dispelled for the entire Universe. That happened in the woods one day. The tail was released just as fast as the comet moved through the sky.

What happened when the ball dropped? When the lead hit? What were your thoughts? There is no telling how the Dark side rejoiced, the same time the Angelic spirit was released.

How many lives have you touched, and still do? Who knows you who never met you? Many I'm sure. Being everywhere at once, using unbounded energy without the need to channel it through your body. How painful, scary and ungrounded you were. It took every ounce of courage to stay here as long as you did. And, every ounce of courage to leave.

BANG. Was it the thunder? No one could tell. Did you want to reach out harder?

Longer? No one answered.

How deafening the silence must have been.

The soul being released takes a little time to transform and recognize no body. "Puff." But your cries out from the ether were heard. You were released. You were freed.

While the rest of us have to eat and poop, it is very disheartening to keep up with it all. Go, be gone. Don't worry about anyone left behind. How much space do I have to hold

for others whose hearts are shattered? A million pieces.

Can they be put together again? Thanks for your help. I know you are the craftsman.

What's left? Tears, sadness, relief, and a belief that you actually made the choice.

I never really felt you had a choice. Though others differ from my opinion.

I personally ditch the Dark side in my consciousness. I don't want it. I don't need it.

I know it must exist to honor the Light. But who cares? Not me. It's years later, and I am missing you. Not the reality, but the physicalness of your beauty.

Your hugs where I'd press my ear to your heart, the heart of the Universe.

The last half hug made me shiver with fear. It is the fear of loss, of the death that seems unnatural, but which is in everyone's face. There is no need to forgive. It's done.

I don't feel gypped like I used to, but in some way blessed.

I AM blessed to have birthed you, to have weaned you, to have kissed you over and over and over. We fought in such an intense way that I am embarrassed to remember. And the love that always came forth was immense.

I know I wasn't the best Mom, but I was learning to nurture, learning to accept, learning to be ok with your ways. It was not easy.

I wonder when I will truly give the space needed for total resurrection of time.

I'm happy to be growing old because it's closer to a time when we can meet again.

I cherish each moment so that I can fully accept life before it is gone.

That feels as if it would be easy. Why do I judge anything? I learned so much from your honesty.

About Janet

Janet was led to study and teach alternative healing and transformational techniques that assisted her in recovering from her own health challenges. She developed a powerful, effective system called The Empowerment Process,® offering private EP healing sessions and intuitive guidance consultations to others in person or on-line.

The premise of the process is that although we cannot change what has happened to us in the past, we can change our responses to those events, and release inappropriate resonances and stuck energy.

As she experienced more refined levels of growth and progress with her clients, she developed a workshop to teach others to become more self-sufficient in healing themselves. Her workshop: "Become Your Own Healer with the Empowerment Process" was developed in 2007.

Since then, she has added two more workshops to enhance the EP Transformational experience: "Balance your Chakras with the Empowerment Process," and "Advanced Tools for EP Practitioners."

Janet's clients include business executives, teachers, professors, medical professionals, healers, theater professionals, parents and children.

Made in the USA
Middletown, DE
17 April 2021

37750306R00106